Fishing for Big Pike

Exploration Fawcett all over again.

RAY WEBB and
BARRIE RICKARDS

Fishing for
Big Pike

ADAM & CHARLES BLACK
LONDON

FIRST PUBLISHED 1971
SECOND EDITION 1976
REPRINTED 1979

A & C BLACK (PUBLISHERS) LIMITED
35 BEDFORD ROW LONDON WC1R 4JH

ISBN 0 7136 1648 2

Reproduced, printed and bound in Great Britain
by Cox & Wyman Ltd,
London, Fakenham and Reading

CONTENTS

ILLUSTRATIONS

FOREWORD

If I judge the situation aright, pike are the 'in' fish of the moment. There has come a new appreciation, a new understanding of them. The old time pike men had that understanding. Then it was lost. Somewhere between the wars, I fancy. But it is back again. One can sense it, particularly in men like Barrie Rickards and Ray Webb, who over the past few years have between them caught 30 pike over 20 lb and 500 others over 10 lb. These figures alone make this book of theirs one we will all want to read.

The next development of pike fishing—after the proper exploration of spinning and plugging and jigging in summertime—will, I believe, be winter night fishing for pike just as the enthusiasts now fish for carp. Barrie and Ray here give the first clear indication of this—with meaningful results.

But for the most part Barrie and Ray have not concerned themselves with the future. They have produced a book about their kind of fishing, the sitting down, traditional English type which gives one time to think, to mull over problems like feeding patterns and hotspots. Their results show how well they have thought.

Barrie and Ray have fished as a team, if not always together, pooling their information. Here they write as a team, each discussing the same question, the one thought complementing the other, a novel approach from which pike men everywhere will benefit.

Bill Keal

ACKNOWLEDGEMENTS

This is difficult. We owe so much to so many pike anglers and even non-anglers. Firstly we should like to thank, individually, the other members of the Cambridgeshire Pike Anglers for their inestimable contribution—Brian Betts of Burwell, Bill Chillingsworth of St Neots, Basil Chilvers of Chatteris, Bill Giles of Norwich, Laurie Manns of Milton, Christine Rickards, Richard and Hugh Reynolds of Cambridge, and Rian Tingay of Littleport. Phil Lane and Mike Holliday assisted with the photography and Peter Collins of *Angling Times* with advice on the MS and publishing. Laurie Manns and Hugh Reynolds corrected the MS, and Christine Rickards typed it. Dug Taylor of York convinced us that you can get more runs than the average bear using ledgered herrings, and Dave Cumpstone, another happy man of no fixed abode, assisted greatly with the Irish piking. There are many other debts which will have to go un-written, but we apologize in advance for any apparent 'name dropping' in the following text—the aim has been to give credit where we think it lies, a procedure often abandoned in modern angling writing! The photographs of the authors on the jacket were provided by Ray Gregory.

PREFACE

A brief survey of anglers of our acquaintance revealed the firm opinion that nobody actually read prefaces: but we need somewhere to explain the manner in which we have written and arranged the succeeding chapters. Apart from the Introduction and Concluding Remarks, for which we are jointly responsible, each chapter is in two parts. The first part, the main part, has the authorship indicated on the chapter headings; and it can be assumed that the second part of each chapter is written by the other author. There is a number of reasons for having a second part to the chapters, but mainly it is to give either an extension of the basic principles outlined in the first part, or a second opinion, particularly on subjects where we might not agree. Chapters containing a considerable amount of instruction are grouped towards the beginning (Chapters 3–9), and are followed by some of the more difficult aspects of piking (Chapters 10–12) such as an appreciation of the effects of weather conditions. Chapters 13–17 are more or less complete in themselves, and are so necessary to anglers who really wish to get *involved* with pike angling in the seventies. We conclude with a 'Blueprint for Success'—a link up of the various topics necessary for the overall, open-minded, approach to the capture of big pike.

PREFACE TO THE SECOND EDITION

For this second edition Ray and I have each added a new chapter. Mine is partly a synopsis of what has happened in the pike angling scene during the last five years, and includes some of the new techniques and theories developed, whilst Ray covers one of the really dramatic changes of the period, namely the fast-changing face of Irish piking involving the swing to bait fishing. We are certain that some mighty pike will be caught during the next few years, and we are certain from the many letters we receive about the first edition that we have managed to fire some enthusiasm for the sport. As we said in the introduction, 'It is our dream that a modern generation of pike anglers will arrive . . .'. It has.

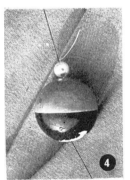

PLATE I

1 Roll up rod holdall with made up pike tackles.
2 "Log" tackle winder for various snap tackles and traces.
3 Hooking arrangement for half baits.
4 Sliding float rig with stop knot, and bead.
5 Homemade snap tackle to rear of deadbait: almost standard rig of B.R.

PLATE 2

1 Brian Allinson stalking pike on a fenland drain.
2 Piking with a Siberian flavour as a blizzard rages.
3 17 lb of pike on the way to the net.
4 Dave Cumpstone trolling with a beach-caster on Killinure Lough.
5 Tinca, anglers' boat extraordinary. Added stabilizers proved a boon.

CHAPTER I

INTRODUCTION

Way back in 1961 on a hot summer's morning on the banks of the larger of the lakes at Carlton Towers in Yorkshire a young student at Hull University and his wife were packing up their tent and camping equipment after a spot of tench fishing which had been productive enough to give that feeling of satisfaction and achievement that only a successful session with the fish can give. Humping enough gear on their back to outfit a full regiment, the young couple were faced with a formidable trudge back to the railway station in the rapidly rising heat of the day, when an extremely weird-looking character, to say the least, came up and offered a lift in his van: accepted unhesitatingly at first but with extreme doubts as to the feasibility on looking inside the vehicle to observe the chaos and disorder within. Completely unperturbed the newcomer would brook no refusal, insisting that there was in fact, 'Plenty of room inside,' and sure enough somehow or other, the trip from the waterside to the station was completed with one driver, two passengers and several tons of assorted debris aboard. Such then was the start of an association that began on the banks of a Yorkshire tench water, developed over the years in common pursuit of a variety of species, and which has reached its maximum enjoyment and fulfilment with the tremendous progress made with the largest of our predators, the pike. It is possible now, with over thirty 20-pound pike to show and reputations firmly established in the angling world, to look back in philosophical vein and ponder the fact that but for the young student's lack of his own transport, this position being rectified shortly afterwards by the way, such a really worthwhile and rewarding partnership could well never have happened and this book too might not have been written.

Two years ago when we were first thinking about writing this book, and discussing the ideas with some friends over a pint in the

White Horse at Milton, someone, no doubt with kindly inten-
tions, remarked that '. . . at least your worst enemies could not
accuse you of being one water–one method pike anglers'. We
remember that he went on to make some less complimentary
remarks about the quality of our tackle, thus identifying himself
in all probability as Laurie Manns of the Cambridgeshire Pike
Anglers, a successful pike angler with scant regard for our rods
and reels, whilst reluctantly agreeing with our general pike-
angling approach. But he raised an interesting point about the
modern pike-angling scene: although a great deal is written
about pike by successful and experienced anglers, all too often
the success and experience is limited to a small geographical area—
even one water—and to a restricted number of methods. When
these methods are applied to other waters, and in other regions of
Britain and Ireland, they commonly fail miserably. The outstanding and stark example is that piking techniques commonly in use
in England are almost a total waste of time on the Irish loughs:
the particular mental transformation required to tackle the
loughs of Eire are dealt with at some length in Chapters 14 and 15
since it is obvious that a vastly increasing number of anglers are
sampling what Ireland has to offer in the way of pike fishing.
Although this is an extreme case the same problems exist at all
levels—two adjacent, apparently identical (even connected)
Fenland drains may demand a quite different approach. In order
to guide the reader we should like to state the limits of our
experience of waters, both in the geographical sense and in the
types of water within one region.

Our serious pike angling began in the East and West Ridings of
Yorkshire, around 1956, after preliminary skirmishes in the
Lincolnshire drains and the Norfolk Broads. East Yorkshire
provides first class pike fishing of a varied nature—deep clay pits
in the Newport area, the Market Weighton Canal and tributary
river, fast rivers such as the River Hull, extensive drain systems
like those we have come to know so well in the Fens, and finally
the glacial lakes, including Hornsea Mere. From all these we had
good double-figure pike to a variety of methods, on big plugs
and Veltic barspoons in the early days; later stationary deadbaits were successful and, less commonly, livebaits; a couple of
fish were taken on streamer fly, and a few more on small bundles
of duckweed dragged slowly across the surface in some shallow

waters. Hornsea Mere, of course, we 'discovered' prior to its Bonanza years of 1964 to 1966, and we probably ruined it as a pike water by our actions, as we shall describe in Chapter 12.

In the West Riding we latched on to ledgered livebait techniques in some relatively shallow waters near Snaith and Goole: on one of these, a circular pool only twenty-five yards in diameter and three feet deep, we had one of our early double-figure pike to a 7 in jointed floating plug after it had steadfastly refused spinners and livebait for over an hour. In this area also we tried innumerable lakes reputed to hold 20-pounders, and learnt the hard way that ninety per cent of angling stories are false, or are so exaggerated that they might just as well be false.

Nineteen sixty-four saw us fishing intensively down on the Great Ouse system, the Fens in general, and with numerous trips back to Yorkshire, and less common attempts to conquer the Broads and the Lincolnshire drains. At about this time we began to travel much farther afield more often: Northmet Pit in London always struck us as the most heavily fished pike water in Britain, that is if one forgets those other London waters like Wanstead Flats. We even tried. a few lakes in Ilford and Brentwood; one other lake at Weald produced some big pike after we had given it up as hopeless!

Nor were Scottish and Irish loughs spared our flashing lures. Lomond remained dour and we did not worry the Irish pike very much at that stage, but they have certainly stopped laughing since. Probably the only waters to which we do not regularly return are those in London and the deep south generally: the numbers of anglers now fishing these waters leaves no room for our dreadful miscasts and verbal accompaniments. Naturally we have wasted a lot of time flitting from place to place, but with three days' fishing each week for fifteen years chosen waters have been given a moderately good trial. We are not masochists and do not believe in spending years trying to crack uncrackable waters: if someone would show us, with proof positive, a 50-pound pike lurking in the depths, we might think about facing a blank outing or two. . . .

So this book is about how to catch pike, preferably double-figure pike (those weighing over ten pounds or, say, 5 kg in the future), and even more preferably 20-pounders. Again, we feel the reader should know something of our results since they

affect two important matters: firstly whether he or she intends
reading the book much further, and secondly whether the various
generalizations made in the book about angling techniques have
much in the way of results to substantiate them.

Perhaps we shall be forgiven for going fishing after writing the
last paragraph: we decided the right sort of colour picture was
needed for the cover, and the conditions seemed good, with
unusual warmth for December on a moderate south west wind.
And a blanket of cloud. *And* a high barometer. So off we went to
a drain deep in the fens, one which we knew was 'on' at the time.
By 11.30 a.m., after four hours' concentrated effort, we were
beginning to regret our decision to fish a water that usually
produced results before 10 a.m. and rarely after that. One of us
remarked ever optimistic 'Must be one of those one-run days,
and that a 20-pounder', and within sixty seconds (honestly)
one small sliding float dropped from the surface, and was not
seen for fully ten minutes. The fish had taken half a mackerel
and was clearly intent on hanging on to it, but as the tug-of-war
began to go our way the pike decided, just before it foamed into
the net, that if she could not have it, nor would we, and the
mackerel was projected skywards in a fair imitation of Apollo 11.
The weight of that pike was greeted with huge matching grins—
$21\frac{1}{4}$ lb. Get the camera out. After some minutes scuffling about
in the bottom of rucksacks and homemade baskets we spun a
coin for who would walk the four and half miles to get the
blasted camera out of the van. One went, the other stayed to
fish on. We needed two good pike, really, if both of us were to
be cover pin-ups. After all it only needs one angler to hold up a
20-pounder, even if it was our seventh since October 1st. By
the time the camera had been set up on a tripod we did indeed
have another fish: a fast travelling $11\frac{1}{2}$ lb fish which fell to a
paternostered livebait. And that was to be your cover picture,
and would have been had the colour transparencies come up to
our usual standards! A minor theme of this book is that there is
always something to go wrong in pike angling, and whilst
photography is normally the least of our worries, this time it just
had to go wrong of course. Particularly after such a good trip
otherwise: the $11\frac{1}{2}$-pounder was followed by one of 16 lb.

However, back to results. That last 20-pounder was our
thirtieth over the magical mark. As we write a 30-pounder

eludes us, as it does most anglers, and our four best fish, shared two each, weighed 29 lb 10 oz; 29 lb; 29 lb; and 28¼ lb. There is often a lot of pleasure in coming close to a target! Twenty-nine pounds of it in fact. When it comes to double-figure pike the situation is quite healthy: we have had well over five hundred and whilst a 10-pounder is a good one anywhere, most waters have them. One of us has had eighty in the past one and a half winter seasons, and the other knocked out big 20-pounders in the heat of last summer.

The generalizations that we make in the following pages depend partly upon these figures. When we make one of the more controversial statements like the fact that pike prefer stationary deadbaits with *few* hooks on them, we can fall back upon whole strings of big pike *and comparative fishing* to back the arguments. We said that the conclusions depend *partly* on these figures. They are also influenced considerably by the results obtained by the anglers with whom we fish—latterly mostly members of the Cambridgeshire Pike Anglers. During the last few years we have, between us, taken over fifteen hundred pike over ten pounds and numbers of 20-pounders. Two recent winter seasons' catches will serve to illustrate:

11 over twenty pounds 1968/69	147 pike over ten pounds
22 ,, , ,, 1969/70	221 ,, ,, ,, ,,

At places in the text where we do not think the facts support the theory—although we *feel* the theory to be correct—we shall try to be careful about saying so. Having stated this, however, we will admit that we hold some views so strongly that we are liable to get bad tempered and arrogant during debate—indeed our views on hotspots and deadbait hooking arrangements are held so strongly, and have been hammered home to us by fish after fish, that we are inclined to curtail discussion by getting the tackle out and going fishing. Which is what it is all about.

What about the modern angling scene? How do we fit in? And more particularly how do the techniques we describe fit into the scheme of things? Probably the big advance one can predict for the future is in the use of artificial lures. This is being pioneered at the present time by a mere handful of anglers. We applaud the move, for not only did our own pike fishing *begin* with big plugs and spoons, but it has continued in the summer months and in Ireland for several years. Our experience with artificials is less than with recent traditional methods of deadbait fishing and livebaiting, but whilst artificials provide exciting summer fishing, the other techniques score particularly well in the winter period from November to March. They also succeed in the summer months. We have, however, briefly documented our experiences with artificials, and particularly with the use of homemade lures on which we have taken fish up to 29 lb in weight. Of one thing we are certain. No single legitimate method of piking is more sporting than any other. Only the angler is sporting or otherwise, and all techniques, including use of artificials, can be abused. We would advocate concentration as the key factor whatever the technique. There *is* a move afoot in angling circles to suggest that use of artificials is the only sporting method of fishing. Bernard Venables, doyen of the modern angling scene, predicted many years ago that this kind of thinking would creep into coarse fishing, just as it did into game fishing. It is of interest that many of those committed completely to the sole use of artificials, actually do very little fishing when the weather gets cold!

We do comment, where we have a contribution to make, upon the various 'moral' questions discussed in pike angling today— deeply hooked fish, heavy pre-baiting, net versus gaffs, summer piking and so on—but more important than all this, it is our hope to contribute something towards the new attitude of mind towards pike and pike fishing. Preparation for pike fishing, both mental and physical, is of the utmost importance. It is a little silly going pike fishing if you have to spend half the day catching livebait; even sillier to restrict yourself to one method of pike fishing. It is our dream that a modern generation of pike anglers will arrive who will put a stop to the ridiculous slaughter of big pike: the inevitable photographs of a pike hanging up in the backyard; the badly stuffed carcases; the pike matches in which the purpose is to remove pike from the water; and the bad handling of pike even by bona fide pike anglers.

CHAPTER 2

FEEDING PATTERNS

Barrie Rickards

There are several facets of pike angling the very existence of which seems to be unknown to many pike anglers. It is most difficult to convince a part-time pike fisherman of the existence of hot spots, or the efficacy of ledgered and free-line livebaits for example. The existence and nature of feeding patterns is another one. This is something the experienced pike man learns to live with, and the reason why he designs his angling so that he can fish for pike from an hour before dawn into dusk: unless he intends night fishing as well. I like an afternoon pottering about at the waterside as much as the next man, and if I get a couple of hours to spare there is no holding me. A lot of anglers, however, do all their piking like that. They will spend early morning until 11 a.m. fishing for livebait, and if they succeed they will livebait for the rest of the day or until the bait runs out. Failing to get livebait they will either deadbait or spin. Usually they pack up about 3 p.m. If the pike on that water happen to be feeding in the middle of the day then those pike anglers may go home well satisfied: very commonly, however, they will have missed the best feeding periods of the day. Conclusions about feeding patterns can only be made by those anglers, preferably with companions, who spend the full day at the water.

Most part-time pikers seem to think firstly that pike are more or less evenly and thinly distributed throughout a water, and secondly that occasionally one of them will feed, and that this could be at any old unpredictable time. All this is quite wrong. It is much more common for many big pike on a water to come on the feed simultaneously, and for the feeding period to last not much longer than one hour, or at the most two. This short active feeding period can be at *any* time of the day, and probably of the night too. It is not my intention to pretend to offer explanations as to why this should be so, but it *is* my aim to convince you that short, exciting feeding periods exist, and that it is during these periods that anglers can expect to catch those 100 lb–200 lb bags of pike, or smaller numbers of really big fish.

October 1st of one recent season found several of us fishing a fenland drain before 6 a.m., that is before dawn. The wind was quite strong, westerly and the weather mild and moderately overcast until late in the day when it became 'cloudy bright'. The barometer had, over a period of several days, been rising steadily: water and air temperatures were more or less constant prior to the season opening and for some time afterwards.

As dawn came each angler could be seen relaxing in the sedges, head only visible, and most of us were employing one rod with float ledgered deadbait and another with paternostered livebait: some were using two livebait rods, both paternostered. It is often as well to fish through the dawn period with a paternoster tackle, and when visibility improves and tactical judgements made more easily, free-swimming livebaits can be used if considered necessary. Not much happened for about two hours save the odd, rash, fenland bream rolling in the waves, but at a few minutes past eight my paternostered $\frac{3}{4}$ lb perch livebait bobbed out of sight and I was in business with a battling, leaping pike, my first of the winter season. Weighed immediately this one went 16$\frac{1}{2}$ lb, and whilst returning it to the water I noticed my second float slide away without so much as a bob. Yet another heart-stopping battle ensued, and just as the fish hit the net I saw Hugh Reynolds a little way down the bank struggling with a big fish. Mine weighed 15 lb exactly, and Hugh's 17$\frac{3}{4}$ lb. I hurriedly got both my tackles into action in the swim again, and in fact, hadn't long to wait before further fireworks. The sport continued non-stop until about 9.15 a.m., and by 9.30 a.m. it was all over. Even though we fished on until almost dusk only one other run was registered. The total for that spectacular 1$\frac{1}{2}$ hours was twelve double-figure pike of 13$\frac{3}{4}$ lb; 15 lb; 18$\frac{1}{4}$ lb; 17$\frac{3}{4}$ lb; 12 lb; 16$\frac{1}{2}$ lb; 15 lb; 15$\frac{1}{4}$ lb; 10$\frac{1}{2}$ lb; 11$\frac{3}{4}$ lb; 17$\frac{1}{2}$ lb and 14$\frac{3}{4}$ lb, totalling 178 lb. A number of smaller fish were taken making the total over 200 lb to four anglers. My own score was seven over ten pounds and one other of seven pounds for a total weight of more than 100 lb.

Almost every fish, and certainly all the double-figure fish, fell within the 1½-hour spell. Anglers arriving at the usual 11 a.m. or thereabouts would have thought the water devoid of pike, and would have continued to think so had they fished the water for the next three weeks. October 3rd saw us take a similar bag of eleven double-figure pike, in addition to smaller ones, again totalling over 200 pounds. My own share was eight fish, six over 10 lb, totalling just under 100 lb, the best fish falling to a half-mackerel, on my rod, weighed 19½ lb. Once again all the fish were taken during approximately 1½ hours between 8.45 a.m. and 10.15 a.m.

This pattern continued for between three and four weeks during which time some superb fishing was experienced: some of the early morning feeding spells, usually lasting 1–1½ hours, were over by 8 a.m. Suddenly things changed, possibly coincident with an obscure weather change, and instead of feeding in the early morning they began activities, less spectacularly as a rule, at about 1 p.m. and finished at 3 p.m. Approximately two hours feeding with fewer fish caught than during the early morning spells and yet the best fish, again falling to my half-mackerel, topped twenty pounds. The afternoon feeding period lasted some four or five weeks when it was followed by a change to midday feeding, coinciding with the first of the real winter weather and the deadly cold dawns.

I have experienced such feeding patterns commonly, both before and since the above examples, and on a number of quite different types of water. Several general conclusions can be drawn. Firstly such short feeding periods hold good for about four to five weeks, occasionally longer, more commonly shorter. It is quite critical, I should think on *any* water, to identify the feeding pattern within two weeks; say, six full day sessions. Otherwise the angler may miss almost all the sport. It is simply no use the angler sticking his head in the sand, saying 'What was good enough for Grandpa is good enough for me', and insisting that big pike can be caught at irregular intervals throughout most of the daylight hours.

There are exceptions, of course. Over and above any feeding patterns of the kind just described some waters are good early morning waters or late evening waters. I know one still water where irrespective of whether the day has been good or bad fishing, the odd big pike can be expected in the last hour of the day: a near-by water is equally good in the early morning from this point of view. And drastic weather changes, such as melting snow water, can completely send fish off the feed. A feeding pattern that has been identified prior to the snow water may or may not be maintained after settled conditions are resumed. The angler may have to start all over again.

Whilst most keen pike anglers I know seem to manage three days' fishing each week, many anglers are able only to fish one day per week. In their cases the chances of identifying the feeding pattern on a particular water are much less, and it becomes quite critical for them to fish from dawn till dusk, preferably using several techniques. Better still is for several anglers to combine their results and experiences.

Individual fish may also be exceptions to the rules that appear to be governing most of their brethren. I suspect it is these fish that the active and persistent spinning men pick up. The top flight spinning man may also partake of the really active feeding spells if he is there at the right time of course, but my own experience is that big pike are more commonly taken on dead and/or livebaits during such spells. A good example occurred on one of our waters a couple of years ago. Basil Chilvers using big plugs had taken several good fish, including pike over ten pounds, when Bill Chillingsworth and Laurie Manns moved in with livebaits. Considerably better results were achieved with the livebaits including a good fish over twenty pounds.

Early morning piking, so alien to most pike anglers it seems, is probably the rule rather than exception, until the depths of winter are reached when midday feeding becomes more common. At the moment the drain I am fishing is going well in the last hour of the day, whereas another stretch on the same water is pretty dead after midday. In the depths of a really cold winter it does seem that the middle of the day is generally quite good. As usual we fish at least from dawn till dusk and I do sometimes wonder if it really matters when they feed. I suppose if you manage to get half a day off work then such knowledge of local or present conditions is invaluable. With a morning spare Fred Wagstaffe tells me he would fish Hickling, and with a spare afternoon he'd probably try Horsey instead, or at least he would have done before all the pike were killed by pollution.

Unless of course he had a strong feeling that he ought to try such and such a swim, or such and such a method. Usually it is impossible to understand or explain feelings like this, but, my word, it is important to give them full rein and not to restrict yourself by 'logical' thought.

Those spells in winter when pike seem to be feeding between 11 a.m. and 2.30 p.m. also explains Ray's magic stove. The angler is beginning to get peckish just as the pike's tum is rumbling too. I well remember us getting three runs simultaneously from a boat on Hornsea Mere, just as Ray had got the chips and onions frying nicely. Ray got hold of his rod, John Neville refused to put out the stove because *he* had a run, and I was at the other end of the punt with a run as well. We could have gone up in smoke on that occasion had not Ray, realizing that two maniacs were in the boat with him, put down his own rod and attended to the stove. Apart from the chaos, I only remember losing my fish in the reeds. I hope John lost his as well.

There was a winter a few years ago when every blasted Christmas cracker contained little plastic trumpets. Quite why these finished up in the tackle bags I'll never know, but suffice it to say that with 12 noon coming up and still no runs registered, four or five of us would line up on top of the bank and blow those trumpets for all we were worth. More often than not we had a run within half an hour. Talk about the walls of Jericho. Of course if you behaved like that today you'd be thrown off the water. And I'll bet we were more musical than the Cambridge group of amateur comedians: it is difficult in the extreme to get any fishing done when out with Reynolds and his shower of merry men.

Moving on to summer fishing there is still a really good case to be made out for early morning fishing, between dawn and about breakfast time. Since the last hour of the day can also be pretty good it suggests that light is a factor to be taken into account. Carlton Towers in the West Riding of Yorkshire used to be a good 'last hour' water in summer and I can remember taking a fair number of fish in the 4–6 lb bracket, usually getting one run per session at this time. I also saw a local man take a fish of 18 lb on a float ledgered dead mouse that he had found on the bank: this fish also took in the last minutes of daylight as I was tench fishing the next swim.

Generally in summer the pike are more spread out and not

usually bunched up into packs, and their feeding habits become, probably in consequence, more individual. I have long felt that this is a contributory reason for the success of artificial lures in summer. (In winter artificials are very much less effective.) This, and the fact that pike feed more often in summer than in winter, whilst heavier weed growth affords them some protection from live baits and static deadbaits. I remain uncertain as to whether the same sharply defined feeding patterns described at the beginning of this chapter obtain during the summer months, and certainly I have not the same incontrovertible evidence to support them. More daylight in summer makes detection of feeding patterns more difficult, for it is a tough character who can fish from dawn until dusk, some eighteen hours in June. The longer daylight hours may also make it less necessary for the pike to feed in such short sharp bursts as they do in winter, although, as I say, I am uncertain as to whether the pike do or do not feed in such a way in summer. Team fishing would provide the answer no doubt.

Team fishing has provided us in Cambridge with quite definite proof of another interesting phenomenom. Whilst it is absolutely certain that on a particular fenland drain all the pike in one stretch will be on the feed from 8 a.m. to 9.30 a.m., for example, it is equally true that a mile away on the same drain fish may be feeding strongly from, say, 11 a.m. to 1 p.m. One angler cannot be in two places at the same time, but two groups of anglers using the same techniques can fish from dawn until dusk in two quite distant localities. There is no question of error in these conclusions, the evidence from dozens of big pike taken being quite overwhelming.

Perhaps I should end this part of the chapter with the kind of exception to the foregoing that we all dream of: the kind of day where, using two rods, we get runs at regular intervals throughout the whole day and amass a huge bag of good pike, and yet have time to fish slowly and carefully, and time to unhook and return the pike before getting the next run. Such a day provided my wife, Christine, with twenty-three pike totalling 200 lb plus, best fish 19 lb, all taken to livebait and suspended deadbait, for an average weight of just under ten pounds. That particular stretch of river usually fished best in the last couple of hours of daylight—but we began at dawn.

II

Having done quite a lot of summer piking in Ireland recently there is no doubt, in my mind at least, about sharply defined feeding patterns at this time of year. On Lough Ree it quickly became obvious that I could put all I'd got into three hours intensive effort then forget it; the rest of the day being a complete waste of time. Seeking out local advice on arrival I was told that dawn was the very best time of all. It wasn't long before I became firmly convinced that the man who told me that had never got up early himself and given it a try. Another, much younger angler, came along and further strengthened this belief by telling me that for two years he'd tried the pike with every bait in his box at dawn before giving it up in disgust. He'd found the spell from 8 a.m. to 11 a.m. far and away the most productive. In three weeks of intensive fishing out on the water every day I too experienced exactly the same feeding pattern. It didn't vary at all throughout the period, not even for one single day.

Moving off Lough Ree on to the River Shannon itself once again I realized early on that dawn fishing was a mistake. Better by far to have a lie in bed for an extra couple of hours so as to be really fit when the fun started around breakfast time. Actually this river fishing saw the fish feeding slightly later and rather longer, 9 a.m. to 1.30 p.m. being the hot spell. The season had advanced a couple of months from July to September in fact, so that could well have some bearing on the slightly altered feeding times. I fished in company with three other anglers and between us we tried all the hours of daylight till the pattern emerged clear and unmistakable; one could flog the same pike holding swims assiduously all day long, for the most part it would be time and effort wasted. Only the breakfast to dinner time period offering any real hope at all.

When Hornsea was going strong I always felt convinced that in the five or six weeks' fishing from the start of the season, October 1st, many more pike would have been taken had we been allowed to fish on into the night; at least until 11 p.m. or so. Unfortunately the rules of the fishery were against this, a frustrating business in the extreme. One could sit it out regularly all day long with no sign of a take as so frequently happened, then just as the light was beginning to fade and the boats had to be fetched in off the water both rods would develop a run at the same time. It takes a man of character, or should I say a trifle soft in the head, to stick to the rule book in these circumstances. We seriously considered all possibilities, bribery, corruption, physical violence, the lot. Anything that stood any chance at all of seeing us still on the water as midnight approached.

Though generally considered to feed largely by sight in the hours of daylight pike do in fact on some waters continue their predatory activities well on into the night. In times of bright moonlight it is often light enough for feeding of course and one theory put forward is that after a moonlight night sport will be poor the following day on account of the pike having gorged themselves through the hours of darkness. There could well be something in this, on occasions at least, for I was talking to a couple of anglers from Manchester recently and they regularly did exceptionally well using homemade plugs on a water near home by fishing after dark when the full moon was up. By and large, on most waters at most times I am sure that far and away the best sport is to be had during the daytime but the position is by no means hopeless for the night-fishing enthusiast. He could take good catches provided he chooses his conditions.

As regards allowing these strong feelings to be a motivating force I sometimes wonder if a conviction that one ought to give fishing a miss for the day and stay at home to dig the garden isn't the best bet of all. I well remember the old alarm clock rattling away just before dawn recently on a morning when the heavens had opened up and rain was coming down in bucketfuls: taking one look outside I turned over and went back to sleep. Awakening again at 10.45 a.m. to find the day bright and clear, not a cloud in the sky, I figured that by the time I'd rowed to the hot swim a full mile or more away it would be all over, the pike having gone off the feed. After some deliberation however, I did eventually head out up the river and before I'd been fishing ten minutes was doing battle with a pike that weighed, on being finally boated, 28¼ lb, my second biggest ever.

Similarly in 1962, fishing a well known Bedfordshire tench lake, a week's fishing in dreadful conditions with the lake cold and full of dirty flood water saw my companion and I somewhat discouraged having only one eel, several rudd and a pike or two to show. Due back home on Saturday I felt inclined to lie in bed that morning but instead hauled myself out at 3.15 a.m. again to totter to my feet for one last bash. No hope at all as far as I could see, it was just a blind stubborn refusal to give in that drove me out there, but a good thing it did as things turned out for a tench of $5\frac{1}{4}$ lb somehow or other found its way to my net. These and many other instances of a like nature incline me towards the theory that the days when the prospects appear to be nil are the ones to really enthuse about. All of which is not to be taken too seriously, for if conditions are all wrong sheer persistence will produce the odd fish, often of considerable size; but for really outstanding sport, with big fish taken in number, all the controlling factors of weather and water conditions, preparation, feeding patterns, etc. just have to be right.

CHAPTER 3

DEADBAITS

Ray Webb

From my first ever day's fishing way back in the primary school days I conceived a deep hatred, based no doubt on fear, of the pike; a day's gudgeon snatching on the Chesterfield—Stockwith canal being interrupted by the advent of a 4 lb jack into the baited swim. For some considerable time it lay there completely indifferent to all our attempts to foul hook it across the back. The all round evil aspect of its appearance and cold malignant hostility of its eye struck terror and distaste into my impressionable mind in so vivid a fashion that it was very nearly a quarter of a century later before I finally grew out of it. Round about 1956 a couple of my regular angling companions at that time, both extremely keen pike men, persuaded me to accompany them down to the Witham, where I was assured that they would show me what top-class fishing really meant. Still very much under the influence of my childhood encounter with the species, I did nevertheless agree to the trip. For eight solid hours we churned the water to foam with our spinners, all to no avail. Perhaps it was as well that we did in fact fail so completely, for I still did not like the looks of the creature and had we taken a pike or two it is highly probable that I should never have fished for them again. In the event we did not only register a blank on this first outing but repeated the dose on the subsequent trip. The one after that also proved unsuccessful and finally I became fired with determination to level the score with this not-so-easy-after-all adversary; either that or I would die in the attempt.

Three or four seasons flashed by, and throughout the winter months we hammered away at the Witham and its connecting waterways. We were spinning most of the time but occasionally we tried a spot of livebaiting whenever a few roach or perch were available. In spite of the glowing accounts of past successes and huge catches confidently predicted by my companions the returns for this prolonged spell of intensive effort were meagre in the extreme; there was not one double-figure pike to show, the best in fact being a 9-pounder taken on livebait from Bardney Lock. Smaller jacks of four or five pounds were not taken in vast numbers at this time either; they too were few and far between. I well remember one spell of seven weekends fishing when I did not register one single run let alone a fish. On the fifteenth attempt however on a really bitter cold winter's day with a biting east wind on Billinghay Skirth, the livebait bung shot under almost as soon as it hit the water. Line was stripped off the reel at a truly alarming rate and with the old centrepin whizzing round I braked the drum with thumb and forefinger, waited until the rod tip had been bent round into an arc and finally drove the hooks with a firm but not too vigorous strike. I was working on the theory I had read in the text-books a thousand times but in practice there was a distinctly audible 'twang' as the float shot high into the air leaving me to reel in the tackle to find that the wire had parted just above the snap tackle. I had read many times of exhausted climbers, numbed with cold, sinking down to their knees and once down finding it far easier to stay there than attempt to get back up and at this point I could so easily have done the same myself. It was in all probability only the rapid downing of a stiff tot of Drambuie that averted disaster. This then was the position arrived at by 1961. Literally no progress worth mentioning after several winters of really hard work and I am convinced that it was only sheer blind, unreasoning obstinacy that kept me going. My original companions in pike fishing did in fact give it up in disgust leaving me to press on alone.

In the autumn of 1961 however I was tackling up the heavy duty gear once again though this time it was on the banks of an old clay pit in Yorkshire instead of the Witham and the bait too was different; a sizeable herring had replaced the small bar spoon of previous seasons and was now an up and coming lure for pike after being publicized by Fred J. Taylor. It was also a new partner I had along with me, this occasion marking the first of a long and still continuing series of trips after pike with Barrie Rickards. He had suggested that I abandon the Witham watershed in favour of the Yorkshire fisheries. This was a move that was to prove its worth time and time again in the year ahead. With one rod out and fishing my attention was focused on tackling up the second. On looking up I saw my float slide slowly along the surface for a couple of yards and then sink down out of sight. A solid resistance met the strike, this in itself was quite an event for me in those days and something of a tussle ensued as an 11 lb pike was hauled protesting to the shore. This sort of weight ensured its classification as a day to remember and the situation was further improved shortly afterwards when I landed another big one of 9 lb. Two such pike in one day was enough to convince me that the ledgered deadbait technique was well worth studying and subsequent events have amply proved that this in fact is the case. It is no magical method answering all our piking problems since it fails completely, and often for no apparent reason, on many waters. Where it does succeed the fish taken are of an extremely high average size. Pike of three or four pounds will and do of course take a full-sized herring. I have seen on occasions times when a ledgered deadbait has produced a jack not much bigger than itself, but it is nevertheless true that as a rule the method yields a lot of double-figure fish with a good 20-pounder from time to time. On so many waters livebaiting turns up 4-pounders in numbers and wastes valuable baits intended for better things. A ledgered herring on a responsive water will usually cut these unwanted jack down in quantity. In addition the availability of herrings for bait is another factor in their favour; very little time or effort is required to nip along to the local fishmonger to pick up a supply adequate enough for a day's piking. When livebaits are in use, especially during the winter months, roach of 4 oz often prove extremely elusive. If pike are moving freely the smaller fish seem to sense the danger and freeze into complete inactivity. Tackle losses too are rare with the deadbait method. It is much a case of infrequent casting and once the bait is out it does of course stay put in one place. With the non-stop cast and retrieve of spinning or the extensive area of water covered by an energetic livebait, if there are any snags about at all it is virtually certain that the angler will get hooked up from time to time, both tackle and temper being lost as a result.

On the other side of the scale it is often argued, especially by spinning and trolling enthusiasts, that the ledgered deadbait results in so many deeply hooked pike that on a water where the method is extensively practised sport can be expected to decline rapidly. Beyond all doubt there is some element of truth in this belief, though not necessarily because pike are dying in large numbers, for it is just as certainly correct that many waters, when subjected to a heavy pressure of angling activity show rapidly decreasing returns regardless of the method in common use. There are numbers of tench waters I could mention where a couple of seasons' hard fishing by a number of rods has been enough to just about cancel out all hope of sport and no one would be so foolish as to suggest that these extremely hardy fish were all dead. From all the evidence available it would seem that two or three seasons of intensive angling is, in many cases, and with many species, just about as much as the water will stand. Having said that, however, I will be the first to admit that the ledgered deadbait technique can be abused, some anglers leaving rods to fish for themselves for quite lengthy spells. The same criticism can be levelled against livebaiting as well though. Concentration on the job in hand is essential of course, but given that, there are two really effective ways of reducing the danger of a deeply hooked pike. Both of these do in practice work so well that they just about cancel out the problem altogether. The first involves the arming of the bait with a number of trebles, four at least, and then a rapid strike in the event of a take. The other needs one treble only but positioned well back on the deadbait no nearer the head than the dorsal fin and it can, on waters where the pike are prone to turn the bait quickly, be right back at the tail. With either arrangement it is advisable to employ a float so that the development of the run can be observed and assessed. I myself favour the single treble tackle and always have a pair of artery forceps and a disgorger in the old basket. Retrieving the hook without damaging the pike is virtually no problem at all. If all pike anglers, novices and old hands alike, could be educated into carrying these two items of equipment at all times, fisheries being ruined as a result of the ledgered deadbait, or any other method, will be ruled out. Any deterioration in sport experienced will then be due to overfishing and not the method employed as has really been the case all along. Heigham Sounds for example was quickly fished out following the publicity afforded it after Dennis Pye's tremendous catches, but no one ledgered herrings there. This could not have been done because the bottom is thickly covered with a blanket of weed and it was livebaiting all

the way. Even so a few seasons of intensive fishing was enough to
see the sporting prospects ruined. A certain number of pike do
die as a result of deep hooking regardless of the method used. I
have even seen cases where spinners have been taken well down
by fast-striking pike but they are very hardy as a species and the
losses are not, I am convinced, enough to have any real bearing
on the issue.

Though herrings are the really well known, most frequently
used deadbaits other species, both freshwater and salt, do have
their uses. In recent years the mackerel seems to be getting
pressed into service and one well-known, highly successful
specimen hunter assured me that on the water where he did his
pike fishing a sizeable mackerel was three times more effective
than the herring. On other waters the improvement in prospects,
if any, are nothing like so rosy, but nevertheless the mackerel is
well worth an extended trial on any fishery. It is somewhat
difficult at times to obtain them small enough for convenient use
as bait. Both herring and mackerel are quite heavy solid baits, the
latter especially so, this being an advantage in obtaining distance
on the cast. When the pike are lying well out from the bank and
no boat is available I can cover fish in these circumstances with a
deadbait without any trouble when a full-blooded cast with livebaiting tackle sees the roach swimming around fifteen yards or
more short of the quarry. On other waters, however, this extra
weight can work against the angler for where a layer of soft weed
covers the bottom a heavy bait will sink right down out of sight.
To overcome this problem a 6 oz roach with swim bladder left
intact can be weighted so that it will sink slowly down, being just
fractionally heavier than the water itself. This will come to rest
gently on top of the blanket of weed without sinking into it at all.
As a bait in normal circumstances the dead roach may not
compare with the herring or mackerel but when there is weed
around it does at least stay on view, offering the angler some
chance of success. Without having given them a trial myself I am
assured by a number of experienced pike anglers that smelt, the
smallish saltwater species that smells of cucumber, will often
succeed with pike when all else fails and I can well believe it. I
know from my own experiments that a sprat of four inches in
length will regularly do the same. It is, I am certain, the size that
is all important and not the hope of a spot of 'cumber that brings

the pike around. On days and waters where the fish can be said to be well and truly off the feed a tiny offering will sometimes tempt them where a larger bait would be ignored.

Another instance where the sprat proves of great value is where a prebaiting programme is being carried out. This is a policy that can in some cases yield dividends though there is, in fact, no guarantee that it will succeed. On a water where the ledgered herring consistently fails to produce results regular prebaiting sessions with sprat can sometimes bring the pike on feed. One south country pit which yielded no runs at all to herring the first year when it was seriously fished for pike saw them swinging steadily away from live to deadbait half-way through the second winter as the prebaiting started to pay off. In Yorkshire a friend of mine achieved a similar improvement on a local reservoir. For a couple of months his herring rod seemed a waste of time but the position improved steadily from then on, one session alone resulting in seven runs to a mere half a day's fishing. Only a mile or so farther up the same valley is another ideal-looking water. It is clear without being alarmingly so, weed-free bottom, fresh water coming in constantly via a stream at the shallow heavily weeded end and twenty-one feet of depth off the dam by the outflow. Bill Bartles remembers taking a pike of 16¾ lb on live-bait ten years ago, but in spite of heavy prebaiting over a couple of seasons my colleagues and I failed to obtain a single run to herring of sprat. This is one of two interconnected waters that have both failed to respond to prebaiting; the other being absolutely stiff with pike that take maggot, worm, or even bread in the summer, but one 9-pounder is the only success to herring that I ever saw there. As I say the sprat prebaiting pays off sometimes but on other waters it fails completely. On Hornsea it was rarely worthwhile bothering the pike there with prebaiting for they took ledgered livebaits from the word go; they really did not need any coaxing.

One of the really difficult problems that crop up with the deadbait method is the extremely fast run from a pike that picks up a herring and bolts off with it at breakneck speed with no sign of stopping. My first experience of these tearaways was on Hornsea in 1964 when I stared goggle-eyed at line leaving the spool so fast that it could be heard whirring through the rod rings. When I struck on some eighty yards of line, and a couple of seconds later, I met with no resistance at all. Before the season was out this sort of thing had happened to me on three further occasions, each time the run being missed. I consoled myself with the thought that small jack pike were responsible; they just had to be undersized to make off at that speed. Early on in the following winter however, on a day that produced a short but frantic spell of activity, John Neville was playing a vigorous 14-pounder at the other end of the boat and I myself was doing battle with an 18-pounder when the now familiar 'whirring' announced that a tearaway had taken the bait on my second rod. Still playing the 18-pounder with my right hand I slammed in the pickup of the second rod and struck with my left hand just as the spool was being emptied of its last half a dozen turns of line and surprised myself by making contact with what was obviously not a jack. After a number of extremely anxious moments somehow or other all three pike finished up in the bottom of the boat. A considerable amount of chaos ensued but order was finally restored and the tearaway weighed in at 20½ lb exactly. Large or small, and they can be either, these tearaways certainly liven things up. The fantastic acceleration of the pike from a standing start is for me one of the most exciting moments in the game.

II

Deadbaiting with a static bait can be desperately slow. Many anglers make no attempt to locate their quarry, but merely chuck out a herring and hope for the best. I had never met Fred Wagstaffe before the first National Association of Specimen Groups Conference at Chelsea in 1967, but we found we were in solid agreement on this issue: there are thousands of anglers throwing out thousands of herrings, half attended, for hundreds of thous-ands of fishing hours. The returns are relatively small, not with-standing the numbers of 20-pounders reported in the angling press. (Have you noticed how many pike weigh exactly 20 lb? Mine usually weigh 19¾ lb!). The fundamental principle behind stationary herring fishing should be to find the pike, if at all possible before casting, and then concentrate on the tackle.

There is no doubt that ledgered herrings result in a good average size of pike caught, but I do recall an interesting observation that I made on the Great Ouse: on this water my smallest pike on herring is 5 lb, and I have had fewer fish for a higher average weight than with livebaits. But with livebaits, mostly ledgered, I have had just as many big pike, with the small ones thrown in to keep the slow spells interesting. I once had a 1 lb jack on one cast and in the same spot on the next cast had one of $23\frac{1}{4}$ lb.

On the other hand there is no need, in my experience, for stationary deadbaiting to be as slow as the Northampton pike specialist Fred Wagstaffe had found it to be on his waters. I remember being amazed during our fruitful discussions at Chelsea to find that his largest pike to this technique was, in 1965, around 6 lb and by 1967, 11 lb: obviously he had been most unfortunate in his choice of waters for there is no doubt at all that on some waters the fishing of static deadbaits is a waste of time.

Ray and I have had some very slow days, probably as a result of doing the job badly. One lovely winter's day in Norfolk we ledgered two herrings each, near some lock gates. The rods dipped towards the water like drinking fowl; the lines hung slackly; the wind was nil and the sun shone. Lunchtime came and went. We had fired the magic primus, but no Aladdin came. We settled back in our chairs surrounded by a vast array of dirty plates, pans, uneaten chips and onions, loaves, fat, and boxes of herrings. We fell asleep. About an hour later we were gently roused by faint gigglings and chuckles and looked round sleepily to find ourselves surrounded by a vast party of students, mostly female, who had come to see the lock gates and the machinery installed therein. The rods still dipped to the water, the lines were still slack, and so everything remained until dark, a fitting conclusion to fourteen hours of pure, immobile, unadulterated winter, sunbathing pleasure.

This is no way to fish for pike of course, even if it is the way that many people like. Fishing the same swim on an earlier occasion with the lock gates wide open and a full flood coming through I rolled two herrings loaded with Steuart multihook tackles around the bottom. It was really hard work involving a fair amount of casting, recasting, and tackle control in the turbulent current and entangling debris, but in very little time I extracted three double-figure fish, the best weighing $16\frac{1}{2}$ lb. One of the best herring fishermen I know, Roy Hatherley of Edgware, fishes two rods, one ledgering which he recasts roughly every hour and one on float tackle arranged so that it drags very slowly through the swim either just on the bottom or just above it (Fig. 1). He then works slowly downstream in a series of arcs

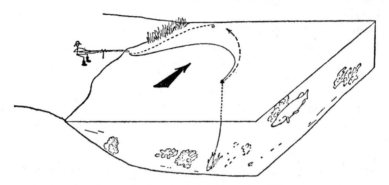

Fig. 1. Drifting a float ledgered deadbait using current or wind drift.

with the float tackle, bringing the ledger rod along behind. The fish that do not like a moving bait often take the stationary one. The hook rig used is the standard Fred Taylor rig of two trebles along one flank of the bait (Fig. 2c). The moral is that unless you are absolutely certain that you are in the swim with a big pike it pays to move slowly and methodically, something after the manner that Roy does. I once remember spotting a pike about 11 lb in the weirpool at Hempholme Lock on the R. Hull, and by a bit of careful work managed to wangle a herring so that it lay on the bottom about six inches in front of the fish's nose. It ignored the bait for about one and a half hours and then, presumably, the smell became too much for it, for it drifted off downstream to get out of the way. I think one and a half hours is about long enough to leave a bait out under most circumstances.

I am confining myself to talking about herrings, sprats and mackerel since most of my experience has been with these easily obtained baits. On the question of large versus small deadbaits— in my case herrings versus sprats or chopped herrings—I think I would have plumped for the whole herrings until 1969 when events on some waters changed my mind about half-herrings and half-mackerels. On numerous occasions we have had a sprat on one rod and I do not really think the returns have been as good as they might have been. Ray has already mentioned the clay pit at Newport in East Yorkshire, where we did a fair bit of deadbait fishing (Fig. 3). Sprats here were a first-rate groundbait, but produced few pike except for a $6\frac{1}{2}$ lb fish that we used to catch once a week. (We would put it in a keep net to stop it going back to eat all the groundbait.) This contradiction suggests that we did not fish the sprats properly, particularly as a number of pike caught on herring were stuffed full of sprats.

As can be imagined we knew exactly where the pike were on this pond and, as on several other waters, experience has dictated our choice of hooking arrangements. In general we found that fewer runs were actually obtained on multihook rigs than on a bait presented with just one treble hook stuck in it. The idea outlined by Ray of having one or two trebles well towards the back of the deadbait, and never nearer the head than the dorsal fin, clearly solves most problems. I was the chief sufferer from multihook rigs, including the Dave Steuart tackle (Fig. 1) for I loved the theory and the whole idea of having plenty of hooks on the bait. I had fewer runs than Ray when fishing in the same swims, and in general finished up with smaller pike. On simple hook arrangements it is rare to get a run and have the pike drop the bait. Whilst the Steuart tackle is a really good rig for well-feeding pike, and I too can say that I have not once missed on the strike when using it, you do get a number of very short, very fast runs which drop the bait like a hot potato. These runs are so fast and so brief that it is quite impossible to get a strike in, even if float tackle is used.

I am also quite certain that a lot of pike pick up herrings loaded with multihook rigs and drop them quickly without producing more than the merest tremble on the float or twitch on the line. On numerous occasions I have found my herrings marked by the pike's teeth and yet no trace of a take has been seen. This rarely happens with herrings adorned with simple hook arrangements (Figs. 2e to g), and once they have made up their mind to take it they do just that, and do not let go until the angler unhooks them. The two popular ideas, that the angler cannot fish a herring badly, and that once the bait is lying on the bottom adorned with hooks nothing can go wrong, are quite incorrect.

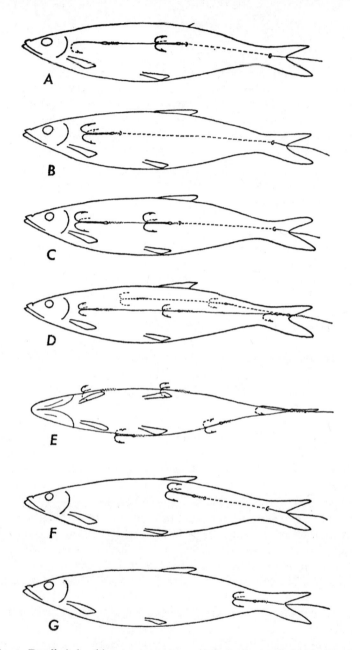

Fig. 2. Deadbait hooking arrangements: A, B; early simple hook rigs used by the authors on Newport Long Pond (Fig. 3). C; 'standard' Fred J. Taylor arrangement. D, E; Steuart multihook rig using small trebles. F; one of the most successful simple hook systems, and one now used almost exclusively by the authors. G; emergency simple rig for the few waters where pike gulp down the deadbait very quickly (see text). In these figures the dashed lines indicate where the trace is *threaded*, except in D where it merely indicates that portion of the trace at the back of the bait.

This is not to say that the pike is super-intelligent, and they probably treat multihook rigs in exactly the same way as do eels, which I have actually seen in action. What eels do is this: they close their jaws on the bait and if they encounter the treble hook, instead of flesh they expect, they simply shuffle along the bait opening and closing their jaws until both jaws feel and taste flesh. Then they take a bite. How often do eel anglers find that their quarry has taken a very neat bite or two out of the bait, exactly between the hooks? The point is simply that they see and smell dead fish, and they expect to eat dead fish, not loads of old iron. Pike-perch behave very similarly except when very small trebles are in use when they will gulp in the lot.

Multihook rigs for pike should, of course, be constructed with very small trebles, at least as small as sizes six and eight. Nevertheless the above remarks still apply—if you want to catch good numbers of big pike, particularly from pike lairs and hot spots (Chapter 12) then forget about multihook rigs. The pike do not like them, and I suspect that even though the pike's jaws are designed to be lacerated (by the very food they eat), they are probably still quite sensitive when feeding leisurely on static deadbaits. For many years I used multihook Steuart tackles on one rod and simpler tackles on the other, but have now completely abandoned use of the former.

Our experiences of far fewer runs on Steuart tackles are not confined to Newport in East Yorkshire, but applied quite spectacularly on the River Great Ouse where four times as many runs were obtained on simple rigs than on Steuart tackles. The test of course is to use the correct Steuart tackle against a simple rig for months in the same swim: there is no doubt whatever about the conclusions to be drawn if the angler adopts this approach. Identical conclusions were reached on Hornsea Mere, where Ray did considerably better than his companions who were using various complicated rigs in the same swims (from the same boat in fact). In this case, and on other waters, it was found that float tackle and leads on the line were also detrimental to success. The shallower and smaller the water the truer this statement probably is, and the simpler the tackle the better the results.

I think the comparative Great Ouse results for part of the winter season of 1965 are useful to conclude this particular

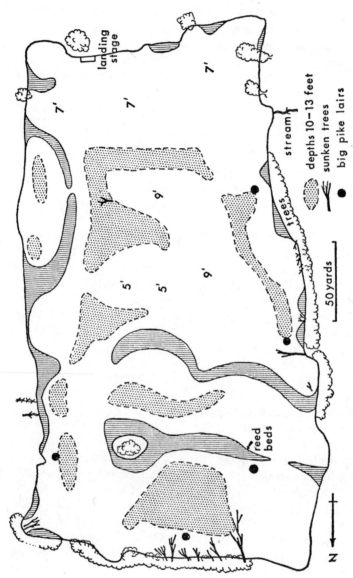

Fig. 3. Newport Long Pond, East Yorkshire. Contouring simplified.

debate, but I would emphasize that the pattern obtaining there is quite typical of other waters and other seasons:

multihook rigs—twenty-six rod days—seven pike
simple rig (single treble)—fourteen rod days—twelve pike

I make the simple tackle between three and four times as effective as the multihook outfit, which more or less agrees with our results on most, but not all, other waters. Some of the possible reasons for this pike behaviour are discussed in the chapter on hotspots and pike lairs, for it is true to say that Ray and I have made a long study of pike hotspots, a concept of which many pike fishermen are completely unaware. The angler who knows nothing of the existence of hotspots will not consistently take 100–200 lb catches of pike.

I am firmly of the opinion that deep-hooking of pike on ledgered deadbaits does not remain a problem for the serious pike angler. The keynote should be attention at all times to the rods, and a reasonably prompt strike once a run is obtained. The number of pike I have caught is in four figures, not three, and of that total only fifteen fish have been badly hooked so that in several cases I had to leave a small treble hook in the throat of the fish. Of these fifteen one took a 7 in long Jim Vincent spoon, and another a large plug—both being standard slack line takes— suggesting that the question of deep hooking does not apply only to static deadbait and livebait fishing.

The only time that deep hooking might become a problem is if a pike hotspot is located where the fish swallow the baits without moving off. Multihook rigs and sensitive float tackles are not the answer here, as some anglers have suggested, for the simple reasons that firstly one is bothered with far fewer runs anyway, and secondly, I have yet to see an angler take his courage in both hands and strike at the merest tremble of his pike float! No, the answer is a simple rig with a small, number six or eight treble hook set right at the tail of the deadbait. I have *never* seen a gut-hooked pike caught on this arrangement. *Always*, there is at least some twitch on the line to give a clue: if the pause after the twitch becomes too long then the angler should gently feel for the pike before striking.

The trouble with all debates about multihook rigs and deep hooking is that, *in theory*, one cannot help but be attracted to the idea of immediate striking. I can only assert that in practice my conclusions, based on our results, are that the subject is a bit of a red herring, and the 'problems' more or less non-existent. The idea in some quarters that herring fishing should be banned, is quite outrageous: education, not banning, is the answer.

There is a very popular idea, connected with the foregoing arguments, that heavy pre-baiting with herrings and sprats cause pike to swallow the anglers' baits without bothering to swim off. In other words that their normal caution has been allayed to a considerable degree and that they just sit on the bottom gulping down whatever is thrown in. This is utterly, completely and demonstrably wrong. The Hornsea Mere pike, and those in Newport Long Pond (Fig. 3) were swallowing herrings without moving off, long before many herrings had been thrown in. The 'problem' was there from the word go, and this has been our experience on a number of other waters, some of which had never seen herrings before. The answer is fairly simple, if not widely appreciated, and merely reflects the fact that the angler has been fishing in an individual pike's lair or in a pike hotspot. On most occasions pike *do* move off after mouthing the bait, but in the particular circumstances just mentioned a fair number of pike may feel no inclination or need to run at all.

How does the question of groundbaiting in general fit into all this? Like Ray I am still in two minds about the value of throwing in sprats and chopped herrings as groundbait. If I did it really regularly, and I do not, then I think I would pre-bait a likely spot when the pike were *off* the feed and had been for several days or more. My hope would be that when they came on again they would have quietly shoaled up in my baited swim There was a time, despite experience in East Yorkshire, when I began to wonder whether pike were really attracted to the smell of herrings. I got over this little mental blockage by setting some traps in Wicken Fen near Cambridge. Some of the traps had chopped herrings in them, others nothing at all. All the traps were set in shallow, weedy ditches, well away from the drain that held pike, but of course connected directly to it. Baited traps of the previous evening were often full of pike the next morning, whereas empty, unbaited traps almost always remained empty. This proved to me conclusively that (a) pike liked the smell of herrings and would move long distances to find them, and

(b) pike are probably much more active at night than is commonly supposed.

Following on from this I decided that instead of baiting up swims with loose offerings of chopped fish, I would put the groundbait in a bag or wire basket rather after the fashion of the sea angler's rubby dubby bags (Fig. 4). This would lessen the risk of one fish mopping up all the groundbait. Every few days I replaced the contents into the swim. The effect was dramatic: the pike moved in and were caught in fair quantity on a water

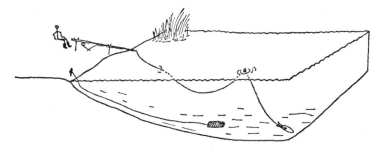

Fig. 4. Using a 'rubby dubby' basket of chopped herrings to attract pike to a swim. Float ledgered deadbait is the tackle in use.

that rarely yielded pike to herring. However, it soon became clear that quite small pike were homing in on the scent, and at one point things got quite farcical with jacks of 1–3 lbs being pulled out regularly. Obviously this idea is open to considerable experiment, and I can imagine it being highly successful on some waters, particularly where small pike are afraid to come out of the weed beds.

So far, I have said nothing about mackerel as bait. My experience of this deadbait is now considerable and I am inclined to believe that Ray's specimen-hunting friend did not exaggerate in claiming mackerel to be three times as effective as herrings on his water. On the waters I fished this year (1970) I have obtained twice as many runs on mackerel as on herring. In fact of the seven 20-pounders I have taken between October 1st 1970 and December 28th 1970 five fell to half-mackerel ledgered at long range. These weighed $23\frac{1}{4}$ lb; 21 lb; $20\frac{1}{2}$ lb; 26 lb and $21\frac{1}{2}$ lb. One fish of $26\frac{1}{2}$ lb fell to half-herring also at long range, and another of $22\frac{3}{4}$ lb to paternostered livebait. The comparison has been borne out week after week with pike ignoring the herrings and yet picking up the mackerels in the same swim. For the time being I am tending to ignore herrings myself!

Mackerel have several distinct advantages over herrings. In the first place they are more solid, less easily broken up, and, in consequence, more easily cast. The hooks tend to take a good hold in the tough skin, and it becomes quite unnecessary to tie the bait on with nylon, crêpe paper, or rubber bands, unless one intends doing some real distance casting. What really interests me is that pike seem to prefer them to herrings, and there is no doubt at all that they have a distinctly more oily appeal than do herrings. The tail end of a mackerel (hooked as in Plate 1.3) really flies through the air. The hook arrangements I have mostly used are shown in the illustration and, clearly, there is no problem about when to strike when using a bait of this size. Assume that the pike is over ten pounds and strike as soon as it is running steadily off. It may be that you are uncertain how much weight your rod will cast. This problem is easily solved with half-baits: simply leave the hooks rather towards the tail and pare off strips until the best weight is found. Choosing the correct casting weight for your rod is much more difficult using whole herrings and mackerels! In fact one often has to resort to throwing the bait out by hand, or using a casting stick.

Half-baits also release a more constant stream of oils and juices which may form a smooth area in the roughest of water conditions. The moment when a pike takes the bait in its mouth is often marked by a vast oil slick bubbling to the surface, giving the attentive angler some warning of events to come. All these factors, and particularly the pike's opinion, have caused several of us to make a marked swing over to mackerel fishing. The only snags are that mackerel are slightly less universally available than herrings, they are more expensive, and they go 'off' more quickly.

Ray has mentioned buoyant baits, designed to sink slowly and settle on soft weed without sinking in. My only experiments so far have been with buoyant mackerels, a state I achieved by stuffing polystyrene and balsa fusiform rods down their throats. The effect (Fig. 5) is to make the bait stand on its tail on the bottom and sway enticingly about. I was not thinking about the weed problem at all, but merely thought they looked attractive

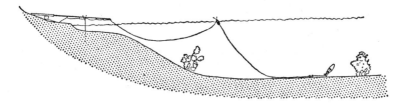

Fig. 5. Float ledgered buoyant mackerel or herring.

when tested in shallow water. I hoped the pike would see the
bait more easily, as well as smell it. The very first cast to this
method produced a hard-battling pike of 14½ lb, and since this
very encouraging start several other good fish have been taken. I
am far from certain that these vertical mackerel are any more
effective than normal ledgered baits on the present evidence,
but suffice it to say that it *is* an effective technique. There is room
for greater experiments with buoyant baits, and I understand
Jim Gibbinson of Essex, and Fred Wagstaffe of Northampton
have used such baits with success to solve problems set by their
particular waters. If I were to attempt a prediction of future
development areas in the broad field of static deadbaiting, I
would probably put buoyant deadbaits and suspended deadbaits
at the top of the list.

All the above remarks are applicable to static, ledgered deadbaits. What of suspended deadbaits? How effective are they?
I have formed a few ideas on suspended deadbaits, and am
constantly irritated by people who say that choppy conditions are
a prerequisite for success. Plenty of good pike have been caught
on suspended deadbait when the water has been flat calm and
the sun beating down, and from my own experience I would
draw no distinction between them at present. On waters where
choppy conditions result in better piking anyway, then presumably this applies to suspended deadbait as to any other
method used.

However, choppy conditions do not result in a suspended
deadbait flapping attractively up and down, except in very shallow
water. Fig. 6 explains what happens in deeper water: the distance *ac* represents the disturbed surface layer in which the
float *c* and the line from *a* to *c* jerks up and down with the wave
action. This happens so regularly and frequently with the wave

action that the line between *a* and *b* (the suspended bait) remains more or less undisturbed, and the bait merely turns round very slowly. The pike knows very well that the bait is stone dead, and I should think the movement of the bait is so slow that it does not attract pike lying beyond the latter's range of vision in the

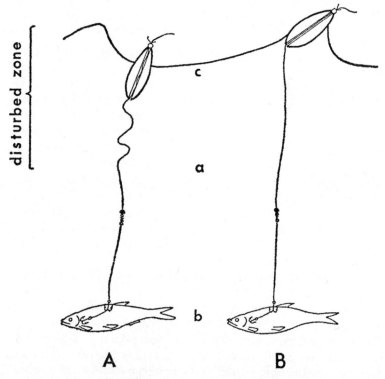

Fig. 6. Suspended deadbait tackle fished in rough conditions.

water concerned. (I presume they can feel vibrations from a greater distance than they can actually see.) No, pike take suspended dead fish because they see a dead fish lying in midwater and they can see no reason for not eating it. If you suspend a deadbait in really clear water, with the sun shining, you can actually see what happens to it even when the surface is quite rough. Only when very near the surface does the bait begin jerking about rather more quickly.

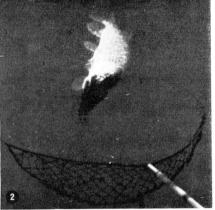

PLATE 3

1 Gagless technique of un-hooking. The left thumb is used to push the pike's upper jaw.

2 Textbook landing of a big pike.

3 Technique of sinking additional tackles, whilst playing in a pike on other tackle.

4 Spring rim landing net. 26″ diameter is capable of dealing with fish up to 30 lb.

PLATE 4

1 Livebait trap.
2 Polythene bait container for a garden pond.
3 Aerated horse trough: livebait store.
4 Bait box providing livebait during a winter freeze up.
5 Livebait tin and anti-splash device.

I have used all types of fish for suspended deadbaits, a half-ounce gudgeon resulting in a fish of 18¼ lb, and a 10 oz roach in a pike of 29 lb 10 oz. The first of these fish was taken only two feet deep in fourteen feet of water, and the second by swimming the stream about 4–6 in off the bottom in ten feet of water. This raises the first point about actual techniques: the pike may be taking in quite a narrow depth band—possibly the depth at which their food fish are swimming—and this may be anywhere from the surface to the bottom in quite deep water. The float needed should be chosen so that it just supports the deadbait weight, or, in rough conditions, should be just large enough to be seen in the waves. Probably I have used more dead roach and bream for this method of piking than any other and wind drift (in still waters) can be used to work the bait and cover the water. By carefully positioning the treble hooks towards the head end of the bait an attractive (to us) sink and draw appearance can be achieved.

But considerable, if not equal success can be obtained by fishing a flat calm still water, with a floating line, and a deadbait suspended below a small float, however unlikely it may seem. Normally we set the deadbaits in a horizontal, so-called life-like position but events at various times have suggested that this is probably unnecessary. Good pike have fallen to baits hanging tail upward or tail downwards! It takes a great deal of faith to fish suspended deadbaits in this manner, but it certainly assists casting. Very little distance can be achieved with a horizontally set bait.

The first time I saw suspended deadbait succeed in calm conditions was many years ago, when I fished a dead perch three feet deep in a twelve foot deep swim in the 'Glucose' lake at Rawcliffe in the West Riding of Yorkshire. Nothing fell to my live baits or plugs that day, but the suspended dead perch slid nicely away and yielded a 4¾ lb jack. A few years later I watched Bill Ellerker, the Hull angler, drifting herrings on a clay pit near Newport. His baits were set at seven feet in eight to nine feet of water, and whilst ledgered herrings, sprats and livebaits remained untouched all day long, the drifted herring contacted big pike twice, both being unfortunately dropped off just as they neared the gaff—a case of too early striking or too few hooks, whichever way you want to look at it. Today, that amount of information would have been enough to start me off investigating thoroughly, for I have learnt the hard way that there is no such thing as coincidence in angling.

A general rule with suspended deadbaits seems to be that the pike are either 'on' them, or 'off' them. Many anglers seem to think that livebaits in the same swims at the same time will always be better but this certainly is not the case. Many a time it has been quite the other way round. Laurie Manns, Christine and myself were livebaiting on the Great Ouse about three years ago, with no success except for a couple of quick tugs. Laurie tried suspended deadbait on one rod and started taking fish regularly. We got the message then and finished up with eighteen good fish between us weighing over 100 lb. None fell to livebaits fished in the same swims and at the same depths. They remained untouched all day long.

It could be added here that this kind of activity is not unique to pike: perch will occasionally take only dead lobworms, and I once shared a large catch of livebait with Rian Tingay all of which fell to dead maggots, live maggots getting only very rare bites. I offer no real explanation as to why pike should prefer suspended deadbaits on enough occasions to make it a useful technique to know, but like so many other piking techniques, the important fact at the moment is that it *does* work well.

The trouble with piking is that there are so many unknowns; and half-baked, shallow theories concocted to explain various pike behaviour patterns, (over feeding and pike swallowing herrings, or rough water being necessary for suspended deadbait) I find rather irritating. Usually such theories are based upon a lack of facts and lack of experience.

Perhaps, purely in the realms of speculation, and in order to encourage the reader to keep an open mind, I can illustrate what I mean by 'unknown factors'. Have you ever spilt a gallon of maggots in the house? Well Christine and I have done just that on three occasions, the last time being in 1967. We arrived back in the evening to find the house alive with maggots in almost every room. After the initial dismay we realized a quite amazing fact—on all three occasions the maggots were crawling round the house in an anticlockwise direction. Presumably, in the southern hemisphere, they would crawl the other way! This is the sort of behaviour I mean—totally unpredictable. How do we know, or how can we test, whether pike will pick up a ledgered herring with the trebles set in its left flank as opposed to its right! In still waters pike might possibly prefer to have the bank on their left, or in front of them, or behind them. The possibilities are endless, and, added to the variables that we *do* know something about, the possible combinations and difficulty of predicting behaviour are probably quite infinite. As I have already waded in up to my neck I think I will retire to the bank and get dried.

Finally what about the 'tearaway' bites that Ray had the temerity to mention at the beginning of this chapter. I think we used to call them 'screamers' at one time. I shall recount just two incidents. One happened on Stow-cum-Quy Fen near Cambridge when I was fishing a water only thirty yards across and forty yards long. As night began to fall I got a little bit drowsy, and I put down the rustling, hissing, sound to the activities of a vole or other animal in the sedges. Only after some time had elapsed did I realize that I had one heck of a run, the line streaming off at great speed. By the time I became fully aware of things about seventy yards of line had been run off the spool. Either the pike was in the cornfield beyond, or else it was running round the little lake in circles. By the time I tightened to the fish it must have done two laps of the lake, and was probably feeling like handing the 'baton' to somebody else, for it dropped it anyway.

Christine had an equally crazy experience at Landbeach Lakes when ledgering herring for the mythical 20-pounder. The run she got was so fast that she dare not strike but sat there amazed and watched a bow wave leave the margin with the herring, run some twenty yards out, turn left round the back of two islands and eventually disappear up the lake still going strong. Finally she did strike and tried to retrieve the two islands with the inevitable result.

CHAPTER 4

LEDGERED LIVEBAITS

Barrie Rickards

On 12 June 1970, my birthday, I was using a very large, black runner eel for pollack off the rocks bordering Clew Bay in Ireland. But all the time I was swinging this artificial bait around—on my pike tackle incidentally—I was thinking what a really superb bait it would make for pike. Needless to say, with this attitude of mind, I caught no pollack. I shall return later on to the relationship of large pike and eels, a subject well worth exploring further: suffice it to say at the moment that the thought of using a small eel on free line tackle dismays me. However, as far as all other livebaits are concerned, free line fishing provides one of the simplest and most deadly piking methods.

It is probably fair to say that very few anglers use free-line or ledgered livebait techniques, despite the fact that both methods are almost always vastly superior to normal float-fished baits. I can recall only two articles in the angling press during the last ten years or so which dealt with ledgered livebait as a technique and none dealing with free-line fishing until 1970, when Jim Gibbinson of Essex began refining our techniques on some large reservoirs. Perhaps it will be of some interest to hear how we came to use the methods in our own fishing. I should preface my remarks by saying that we did not discover these methods—I believe that both are described somewhere by Bickerdyke himself.

As always Ray and I arrived at our findings by the wrong method. What we should have said was that since rod, line and hook are basic to all other methods of fishing (fly fishing, spinning, specimen hunting generally) why not pike fishing? In fact, I *began* by using small ledgered livebaits on Carlton Towers in West Yorkshire quite a number of years ago. This was summer piking, and the problem was to get the bait well out into a small hole in the weeds and to hold it there. The first surprising fact was that the livebait, provided it was under 4 oz or so, did not pull line off the reel but sat quite still on the bottom. I later confirmed this on the Market Weighton Canal in the East Riding where I was able to watch the bait 'in action'. The second most important factor was that the number of pike taken increased fourfold. I attributed this, at the time, to the fact that I had placed my bait exactly where I wanted it and where it remained relatively weed-free. Encouraged, however, I began using ledgered livebait all over the East and West Ridings of Yorkshire in waters varying from deep clay pits to shallow weedy waters.

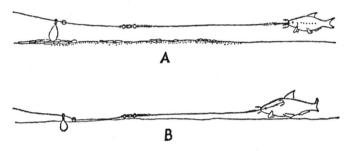

Fig. 7. Lip-hooked, and snap tackled ledgered livebait tackle. The method illustrated as A is preferred by the authors.

I now know that most of the waters I fished did not contain big pike. Nevertheless the *numbers* of fish taken were far in excess of the numbers caught by other anglers fishing the waters at the same time. Let me hasten to add at this point that where big pike *are* present the method is still very effective when compared to the more usual approaches. Nothing fancy is required in the actual makeup of the tackle (Figs. 7 and 8). An Arlesey bomb or swan shot ledger slides on the line and is stopped with a shot fairly close to the normal wire trace. The bait should be lip-hooked: if hooked near the dorsal fin it merely lies on its side on the bottom. If a treble hook is used several small livebaits can be used at the same time, giving the effect of a small shoal of fish.

When I first demonstrated ledgered livebait to Ray on the Great Ouse we were having a rather slow day, and by 4 p.m. we hadn't had a single run on herrings. We then sent my wife, Christine, to a near-by drain to catch some livebait. She quickly bashed out half a dozen smallish roach and suggested that we tried ledgered livebait. The first cast produced a 12 lb fish to my rod. Ray, duly converted, evolved the free-line technique in a matter of days by the simple process of getting rid of the lead altogether (Fig. 9). One of the difficulties with ledgered livebait, you see, is that the lead weight very often finds the snags particularly when a fish takes.

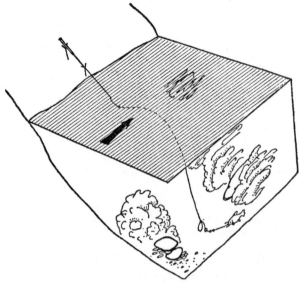

Fig. 8. Holding a ledgered livebait in position in a snag-ridden swim, and moderate current conditions.

On one of the early sessions at Carlton Towers my chosen swim was a mere 18 in–24 in deep, liberally dotted with soft weeds, and surrounded by dense *Potomogeton* and *Elodea* beds. Several traditional livebait bungers had been through the swim during the day, including myself, and a fair bit of spinning had been carried out. Ten minutes after casting out a small roach, lip-hooked, and with a half ounce Arlesey bomb on the line, I got a real sizzler of a run. The pike took about ten yards of line before I caught up with it mentally, banged in the pickup of the Triplex reel and struck violently. There was a boil and explosion of spray deep in one of the weed beds, and the Arlesey bomb shot up into the air at least eight or nine yards away from the fish! Everything, but everything, got tangled up in weed, but after a lot of heaving and tugging, my first pike to ledgered livebait, on my first cast to that method, finished up on the bank. I had another four fish out of the one swim that afternoon, all to the same technique, largest 4 lb; no other pike were taken on the water all day.

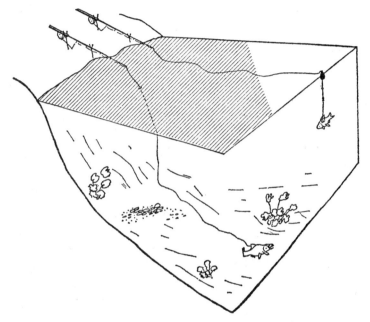

Fig. 9. Free-line livebait tackle (nearest) and 'standard' shallow fished, suspended livebait using a floating line, and *small* float.

It seemed to me at the time, and on subsequent equally successful trips, that the pike in such shallow water were frightened of huge bungs and huge splashy spinners. Later experience with other piking techniques, such as ledgered herrings, bears this out. It *pays* to be as simple as possible with tackle arrangements, and as quiet as possible on the banks. Occasionally, even fairly commonly, such care doesn't matter, but mostly it does and I'm careful all the time as a matter of course.

Free-line tackle hardly demands illustration since the reel line terminates in a trace and hook, either treble or large single as preferred (Fig. 9). Obviously free-lining is carried out at short range up to, say, 25 yards. If more distance is required, or if the current is too strong, it becomes necessary to revert to ledgered livebaits. Addition of a swan shot ledger can be carried out without unshipping the gear although, indeed, this is easy enough! If a few float rubbers have been threaded on the line initially a float can be added if required. There is no doubt in my mind that free-lining produces more and better runs than does ledgered livebait: both are superior to float-fished baits when the pike have been accurately located but are not necessarily feeding strongly.

All livebaiting methods produce their share of 'killed' baits. This occurs when a fish swims up to the bait, clamps on it hard and then immediately drops it for no obvious reason. I have watched this behaviour on Wicken Fen in Cambridgeshire and it really is an astonishing sight. Sometimes a pike will kill a bait, swim away for a few yards, and then turn round and take the (now) deadbait without further hesitation. This is as true when ledgering as it is of float-fished livebaits. For some reason possibly connected with resistance, 'killed' baits are less common when free-lining than with any other method. In Chapter 12 I shall return to the contrast in behaviour between pike which are in their lair (for want of a better word) and pike which are actively hunting whether singly or in packs. I mention it here since in my experience the greatest number of 'killed' baits (that is, without a run developing) occurs when the angler is fishing in a pike's lair. The fact that pike *have* a specific lair can be easily established by the frequency with which a fish, returned to the water, is caught again in the original swim even though this may be hundreds of yards away—in the case of one Hornsea Mere pike almost a mile away. It seems reasonable to me that a pike in its lair, not really hungry, would object to a precocious little roach swimming about and might be expected to deal it a fair old chomp—and then leave it until it was hungry. Or until the eels found it, which then raises other possibilities concerning pike, eels and night fishing!

One or two points might be emphasized on the subject of ledgering and free-lining with relatively small fish. Firstly, when free-lining in either shallow water or deep, still water or running, the bait always behaves in the same way—it swims to the bottom. This immediately overcomes one of the piker's main problems namely that of getting the bait down to where the pike are *most* of the time. Secondly, any of the usual bite indicators can be used—silver paper, electric bite alarm, empty spool etc. As free-lining is done at short range it is rare to get a take which does not give a visible indication. I have not fully explored the use of large livebaits on free-line tackle but my experience at the moment is that bream of half a pound or so either continue to pull off line quite strongly or else rapidly go to weed. Bream are of course first-rate livebaits, every bit as good as dace in my view, though I cannot comment on that reputed good bait, chub. If I had to pick one type of livebait only I'd plump for a bream of around 6 oz. For a start they look bulky for their weight. More important, on the Great Ouse and some Irish Lochs, the pike follow the bream shoals. Pike, unlike many anglers, love little bream.

Earlier on in this chapter I noted that if a ledgered livebait is fished on an ordinary snap tackle, or is hooked near the dorsal fin instead of in the upper or lower lip, then it merely lays on its side on the bed of the lake: a most unlikely way of getting results, and one we condemned as useless.

That was the position until the 1969 winter season when Hugh Reynolds began fishing the ledgered livebaits attached as nor-mally to a simple snap tackle. As predicted in the last paragraph the baits lay quite still on the bottom, on their sides in fact. But this did not stop him getting some perfectly sizzling bites and some very good pike, the best, if I remember rightly, going well over twenty pounds. Those fish were taken in eight feet of water at fairly close range, say less than twenty-five yards, on a still-water near Cambridge. More important, however, they were caught at a time when the usual ledgered herrings and float-fished livebaits, fished in the same swims, produced little in the way of success. Hugh's pike had an average weight, in the first three months of that season of 19 lb, a feat I have never before or since seen equalled. And the average was based on more than a handful of fish!

A further point, which we hardly dare mention these days, was that the water in question had rarely produced fish to ledgered livebaits previously, and had joined the short list of still waters where the technique seemed to be a failure. Unfortunately we have not had the opportunity this year to extend Hugh's experiments, but the instance serves to demonstrate that the pike angler must try to remain open-minded. I remember remaining quite surprised for some years that pike should bother with a livebait that 'sat' so quietly on the bottom, rarely moving more than a foot or two. So why should I be surprised at Hugh's unlikely technique? A parallel might be drawn here with suspended deadbait fishing: we always try to fit the deadbait in the horizontal 'natural' position and yet I've had a fair number of pike when the deadbait has been hanging head downwards *or* head upwards! A most unlikely arrangement one would think, but it works.

What about bite indication on ledgered and free-lined livebaits? This is a question which worries many possible converts. Surely, they think, a free-lined livebait results in numbers of gorged baits? It does not. Remember that free-lining is usually done at quite short range, and even when the feeding pike moves in towards the bank one either sees the line trickling steadily off the spool, or else a clear slack-line bite ensues. Slack-line pike takes should be treated as positively as slack-line bites obtained when chub fishing, except that when piking one feels for the fish first then belts it.

All the usual bite indicating paraphernalia can be used: silver paper, empty line spools, sticks, buzzers, and any other you care to invent that allow the pike to take a little line before the strike is made. It is of interest that we always allow pike to take with as little resistance as possible, and in this respect free-line and ledgered baits score heavily, even over streamlined float tackle; and yet the Irish long-liners take both pike and eels in quantity and quality on their fixed lines. I suppose the point is that we do not know how many pike drop the long-liners' baits on feeling the resistance. But how many pike anglers have tried a tug-of-war with their quarry? I certainly haven't the nerve to try it: when a run occurs it might be a 30-pounder and I'm taking no chances at all! Of course, the idea could be tried on a water where the pike are small, but then the same arguments would apply when we came face to face with pike on a big fish water. If, however, such a technique were successful it would presumably eliminate even the faint possibility of deep hooking (or would it?) and it would lessen the risk of snagging on ledger tackle.

Still further on the subject of ledgered livebaits and resistance, we have spent some time recently on a water where big pike will happily carry up to two ounces of lead without dropping the bait. We first noticed this using paternoster rigs, but since then I have used fixed one ounce leads on ledger tackle with some success, the best fish to date being 14 lb. The great advantage of a fixed lead is that it makes longer casting very much easier and smoother, the tendency to cast the livebait 'though the lead' being quite eliminated. An open-minded approach to these 'resistance' techniques might produce startling results on some waters. Perhaps we can expect advances in ledgered livebait techniques in other directions. Jim Gibbinson, our Essex friend, and well-known pike fisherman, has evolved a method of twitched live and deadbaits. Weed-free hooks are used and the bait is twitched only an inch or two at a time back to the bank. The weed-free effect is achieved by fixing stiff nylon bristles or pieces of Alasticum wire from the point of the hooks to the shank near the hook eye. The attacking pike easily closes the bristles and exposes the hooks. Clearly, as with stationary deadbaits, there is every possibility of varying one's method of fishing from the truly 'stationary' methods to the truly 'mobile'. To date we have not experimented with these latest methods, because the simple free-line or ledger methods are getting results.

II

My own introduction to the use of ledgered livebait took place in 1964. Prior to that time I'd unquestionably followed the traditional technique of suspending a bait off the bottom beneath a bung. For three years or so I'd been growing increasingly enthusiastic about ledgered deadbaits so it ought to have dawned on me earlier that a livebait fished on the bottom might also prove a winner too; there were in fact times, when, put to the test, it left the traditional style standing and the herring too, come to that. One water I used it on fairly extensively was a river with a very gentle flow. It worked out far more effectively than a suspended livebait, yet the same water, only two or three miles farther downstream, passed through a sluice, and here ledgered livebaiting became a waste of time. Here the ledgered livebait, though it did produce the occasional fish up to 23¾ lb in fact, ran a very poor second indeed. Just what happened at or below the gates to account for this I could never make out; it certainly wasn't increasing weed growth that obscured the bait for there just wasn't any and the depth too was pretty similar. It seemed to be just another of the innumerable instances which go to prove just how little we really do know about this angling game of ours, no matter how long and diligently we study.

A bait that can also come under this classification and one that can at times prove very effective is the lobworm, fished singly or in numbers. I've seen a number of waters where this seemed to be the best bait of all. My own first double-figure pike taken in 1957 before I even started fishing for the species came to a lob being ledgered on the bottom in hopes of contacting the big perch of an old gravel pit near Newark on 4 lb line without a wire trace. It was quite a prolonged battle before the 13 lb 1 oz pike was hauled up the bank. It was no isolated freak whim that prompted this fish to take my bait either. It had taken my companion's worms three or four times earlier the same day breaking him up rapidly on each occasion. All this happened on a day when livebaiters and spinning men were flogging away at the same water, hour after hour, without any response at all. Many times after this, on a variety of waters, I've seen the lob taken by a good pike when all else failed. It's a surprisingly effective bait, especially on canals where it will so often prove streets ahead of anything else the angler may care to offer.

CHAPTER 5

OTHER LIVEBAITING TECHNIQUES

Barrie Rickards

As the reader will be aware by now we do not spend a great deal of time 'bung' fishing for pike; that is, using a large float fixed a short distance of two to three feet above a (usually) small livebait. However, if it becomes necessary I will use such techniques with the best of them and before going on to discuss more sophisticated methods of float-fishing livebait it might be a help to describe some circumstances where the traditional method actually works quite well. This is in solidly weeded waters.

By this I mean shallow waters where the surface is weed from bank to bank, whether it be *Potomageton* leaves at intervals of a few inches or thicker, softer, weedgrowths. Pike live quite happily in waters like this, and, as usual, manage to reach double figures or even twenty pounds occasionally. I think we can learn a fair bit by watching and catching pike in weeded waters: the fact is that in many waters pike often hunt right in the thick of the weeds and not merely round the fringes of weed beds. This is where the angler fishes, and there is a world of difference between what the pike like and what anglers like.

Up in Yorkshire we used to fish the *Potomageton* beds at East-rington pits near Howden with thick line, a large bung set only three feet deep, and a snap tackle and livebait (Fig. 9). The procedure was quite simple: we heaved the tackle into the weeds. And we caught plenty of pike which were landed trailing ten-feet lengths of weed stalks in their mouths. It is quite natural for pike to hunt in these conditions and I think this is why pike in general are less suspicious of thick lines, large hooks, resistance and even keep nets, than are other fish. But a pike only needs to see you once, or be frightened by a heavy footfall or dropped oar, and you can usually say goodbye for a while. I have always advocated a far more cautious approach to piking

than is practised by most anglers. And remember too that a pike
does not always charge away when it has been scared. If you
watch closely a fish that has definitely seen you, the very edges of
the dorsal fin can be seen to make minutely agitated movements.
The fish is keyed up to go, and at the next violent movement
which you make, it does just that.

There are other occasions when I would use a shallow-fished
live (or dead) bait, but not under a large bung. Those are the
times when big pike are feeding very close to the surface over
deep water. The line is set to float by rubbing it with 'Mucilin',
and the smallest float needed to support the bait is set *sliding* on
the line even if I intend fishing less than two feet deep. But how
does one fish sliding pike floats? It is my intention at this point to
describe what I think is one of the most versatile livebait tackle
rigs in existence, an outfit that whilst being thoroughly efficient
in its prime purpose, can also be very quickly adapted or changed
to suit most livebaiting problems.

Assuming that the rod has been put together and the line
threaded through the rings, the next requirement is a stop knot
on the line set roughly at the depth to be fished: it can be adjusted
when the whole rig is assembled. Stop knots made of rubber
bands soon perish, or work loose, and the best material is either
nylon monofil about 6 lb b.s., or thick cotton (Plate 1.4). I have
used nylon monofil for years and the only drawback I can think
of is that if pulled too tight it tends to weaken the reel line, by
decreasing its diameter locally. The knot itself is crude but
effective: simply tie one granny knot after another until the
bunch of knots is rather less than the size of the pin head. Practice
determines how tight to set it—about three minutes' practice in
fact! The loose ends are then cut back to about 1 in lengths
which tend to stand proud of the reel line. A stop knot of this
kind flies easily through the rod rings, unlike one made of rubber
band, and if well tied in the first place can be left on the reel line
for weeks or months.

If you are a particularly fastidious person with strong objections to scruffy knots, then the standard Billy Lane sliding
float stop knot can be used instead. To make one of these,
requiring a little more practice perhaps, a loop of 6 lb b.s. line is
laid alongside the reel line, and then one end is coiled around the
loop five or six times before passing the same end through the

remaining part of the loop. The other loose end of line is then pulled tight, and the fingers used to carefully control the shape and tenseness of the knot. The end product is a relatively long knot of coils, with two loose ends which can be trimmed down as before.

Cotton knots may rot before several months have passed but this hardly seems a serious criticism of them! The cotton is rather easier on the reel line than is nylon monofil, but does not stand proud of the reel line when trimmed. However, the same bunched-up knot can be constructed and in the arrangement described below it is not necessary anyway to have stiff ends of the line built into the knot. I shall preface further remarks by saying that the kind of detail I am describing here, reflecting an attention to detail in my own fishing, is critical to successful pike angling. There is nothing sillier than having the depth fixer go wrong just when the pike are coming on the feed in a narrow depth band.

Having fixed the stop knot the next job is to slide a small bead, say less than a quarter of an inch in diameter, on to the line. There are beads and beads and beads, and you can safely assume at the moment that the ones sold in fishing tackle shops are unsuitable. Almost all of them have too large a hole through them, and in any event the tackle shop beads are probably sold for constructing spinners. I get my beads from Woolworths by buying a 'pearl' necklace of several strings' width. The cost is quite modest, and the necklace yields hundreds of beads from quite small, say one eighth of an inch in diameter, up to a quarter of an inch. The hole is exactly right for nylon monofil breaking strains from ten to fifteen pounds. Slightly larger holes can easily be made if required by working them with the point of a treble hook. Briefly test that the bead is stopped by the knot, though it becomes second nature after a while to get it right first time, and you are ready for the float.

Mostly the floats we use are one inch and two inches diameter; round floats with a hole straight through the middle. No slits or wires are needed: the stop knot arrests the bead and the bead stops the float. However, the beauty of this system is that any old floats you may have, or may find on the bank, can easily be converted, or even used directly, for the simple reason that the diameter of the bead is usually much greater than the diameter of any wire rings or loop attached to pike floats. *Fishing Gazette* floats can be converted by gluing cork in the slit, or more quickly by sticking a pin across the slit (Fig. 10). The line is then threaded through the centre hole and the pin stops it slipping out through the slit. Laurie Manns was responsible for that brilliant little conversion idea.

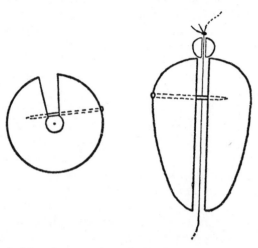

Fig. 10. Laurie Manns' conversion of a *Fishing Gazette* float, using a long pin, to turn it into a sliding float.

The basic principle with floats is to use the smallest you can get away with under the conditions. Rougher conditions than usual, stronger currents, and larger baits may all require the use of bigger floats. Two small ones can be used, both sliding quite freely on the line utterly independent of each other. If I am using a two inch diameter round slider and decide more buoyancy is needed I merely slide on a one inch diameter float underneath it. Larger floats I carve out of balsa or use crude corks, and push holes through either with a knitting needle or some other pointed object. When using single larger floats they might just as well be long and streamlined, that is, with the fat end pointing into the water, and not, as sold by so many manufacturers, with the pointed end downwards. Think of the cross section of an aeroplane wing—fat edge into the wind.

It is as well to have a variety of colours in the float box. Dark green or black can be made the 'lower' colour if you like two-tone

PLATE 5

(*above*) 29 lb 10 ozs. to large suspended deadbait.
(*below*) Christine Rickards and Laurie Manns display Christine's 200 lb
plus bag of pike to 19 lb.

PLATE 6

1 26½ lb taken long range on halfbait.
2 20½ and 26 lb on successive casts. Tackle: long range, half mackerel.
3 Getting it taped. Measuring the girth of a dumpy 20 lb fish.
4 An example of the rare kyped pike!
5 Most two-tone pike are 3:1 in quarter segments. This is the only half and half two-tone fish to date. Bright yellow in the front. Fish of 13 lb.

floats: these can then be turned upside down when light conditions demand a dark float. Fire orange and yellow are two all-round colours for the float top, but white ones are useful sometimes. Providing one sticks to the basic idea of choosing the smallest float for the job, this business of float shape and colours is definitely of secondary importance. For one thing light conditions change so quickly in winter that it becomes a bit of a fiddle changing floats.

Below the float, at varying distances from the wire trace, I pinch a swan shot which prevents the float from sliding down, during casting, over the swivel to the bait and hooks. And lastly there is the trace and hook system itself. There is, of course, an almost infinite variety of possible hook arrangements, and many possible trace materials, but the tackle I now use a great deal is the oft-maligned snap tackle designed so many years ago by Alfred Jardine. It is surprising, in view of the awful hammering the snap tackle has received from angling writers, that many experienced pike anglers came back to using it after trying and rejecting many other outfits. Dennis Pye, I believe, has always used them and I remember Bill Chillingsworth and myself reverting to using them several years ago after years of single treble rigs, and multihook rigs.

Snap tackle hooks should be small, sizes six and eight, the trace wire fine, preferably dark-coloured, and supple. Shop-bought snaps rarely measure up to these requirements, probably most brands being much too thick in the wire of both trace and hooks. It *is* possible to buy snap tackles on fine wire, Stiletto being one make, but they take some finding in all except large tackle shops. Yet other snaps have much too short a trace wire: a 30-pounder could gulp down the whole rig, and this is something I am just not prepared to risk. So many other things can go wrong during piking that we may as well iron out the problems over which we do have some control. So I now make my own snap tackles of cabled Alasticum wire, size six and eight trebles, and size six and size eight Ryder hoods. A swivel at the other end completes the tackle.

It is not widely appreciated that Alasticum wire can be obtained in the cabled state. It is pointless to quote prices in time of inflation, but a cabled roll is shorter than one of single-strand. The cabled form is superior in several respects: it is thinner and more supple, retains its dark colour indefinitely, and kinks much less easily. Hooks (except the Ryder hook) and swivels can be attached either by using brass crimp-on sleeves, available in most tackle shops, or by twisting the Alasticum. The last method is perfectly adequate: Basil Chilvers tried it first, amongst my own angling companions anyway, and swiftly converted us from crimp-on sleeves even though we had never had these fail us.

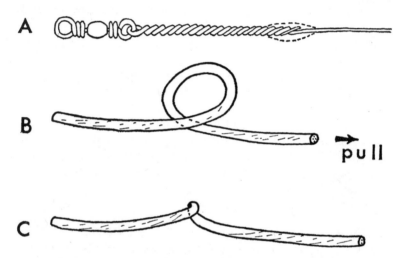

Fig. 11. A; cabled Alasticum Knot: dashed lines indicate position of small blob of Araldite. B, C; the way in which dangerous kinks develop in Alasticum wire.

Richard Reynolds adds a spot of Araldite resin to the end of the twisted portion (Fig. 11a) thus lessening the risk of the connection untwisting. However, it never does untwist! The Ryder hook is slid into position *before* the swivel is attached. Suitable trace lengths are about twelve inches, although they can be longer if preferred. Traces should be ruthlessly abandoned to the tackle box if they become kinked in the manner depicted in Fig. 11b, c. The effect of such kinks is to reduce the breaking strain of the wire by about 80 per cent, and whilst single-strand Alasticum is even more prone to such kinds, it *does* happen fairly often to the cabled variety.

Most other types of trace wire sold are much too thick or shiny, or both. And there is one kind, plastic-coated wire, which looks most attractive in the shops but which is useless for anglers who go pike fishing more than two or three times a year. At the slightest provocation from pike's teeth the plastic shreds off the wire, the whole approaching a close resemblance to 'Hairy Dan' string.

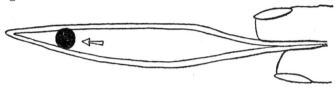

Fig. 12. A way of taking out a less serious kink in trace wire than that depicted in Fig. 11c, using a round cross-sectioned object such as a ball-point pen. Not to scale.

To sum up then, we have now 'built' a very good tackle arrangement with a sliding float, stop and bead, swan shot, and at the bottom a snap tackle with small hooks and fine wire. What can we achieve with this rig? Firstly it is possible to fish simple free-roving live bait at *any* depth. The stop is more easily slid along the reel line when the latter is wet, so a short false cast (without the bait) is made on to the water and the tackle retrieved. The exact depth required can then be set: I use the five foot rod joints as a reasonable guide. The Dennis Pye system of fishing the reedy margins of shallow Broads-like waters can be carried out by setting the float from twelve inches to two feet deep: a dumb-bell float can be used if preferred, although I have never really been able to understand the theory behind the use of dumb-bell floats.

Should the angler wish to change from fishing a two foot deep marginal swim, to searching a twenty foot deep hole, the adjust-

Fig. 13. Paternostered livebait tangling a sunken line.

ment is made in seconds. When fishing a free-moving livebait in deep water the line does not have to be floating since there is much less chance of the bait swimming upwards and crossing the line above the float (see Fig. 13). On the other hand if drift is required, then it is a matter of seconds to retrieve the line through line grease in a rag held in the right hand (assuming the angler to be right-handed): the right hand with the rag is held up towards the butt ring, that is not too close to the reel, since this makes winding in more difficult.

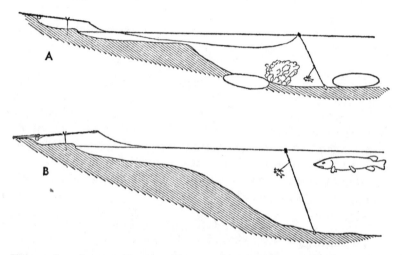

Fig. 14. A; using paternoster tackle to anchor the bait in snag-ridden water. B; paternostering near the surface in deep water.

Paternostering with float tackle (Fig. 14) is easily carried out by tying one end of the required length of six pound (weak) line to the trace swivel and adding a weight to the other end. In order to fish five feet off the bottom fit a five-foot long to six-foot long paternoster, and shallow the stop shot by five to six feet. Three way swivels are quite unnecessary and get into just as many tangles as the tackle described here (Fig. 15). Tangles are in fact relatively uncommon except with rudd livebaits fished in still water. Quite recently I saw in an angling magazine pike feature the statement that rudd are not lively baits. How anyone could ever come to such a conclusion is beyond me: they are the only baits that tangle up paternoster rigs, and they do not do things by

OTHER LIVEBAITING TECHNIQUES

halves either. If any stream at all is running there are very few problems with paternoster tangling, and, when casting, both bait and weight tend to stay quite apart.

Paternostering can be used in many different circumstances such as very shallow drains on the one hand to deep gravel pits on the other, and is particularly useful when it is necessary to hold

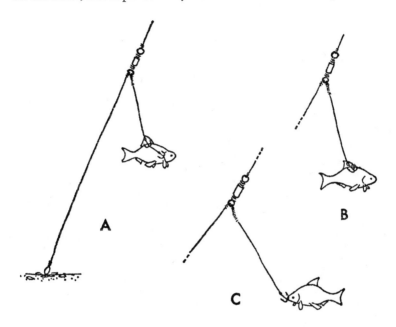

Fig. 15. Paternoster rig detail, using a simple swivel (or trace wire loop) with snap tackle (A), single treble near dorsal fin (B), and lip-hooked livebait (C). Not to scale.

the bait in one spot. It may be, for example, that the current tends to push a free-moving livebait a little bit *too* close to the bank, or the weed growth is too thick for comfort. There is one swim that my friends and I often fish where it is necessary to somehow anchor the bait about six feet off the bottom and within two feet of an old wall. If it drifts away from this exact spot it works its way into snags, and away from the big pike in fact: so far this tiny area has yielded fish of $28\frac{1}{4}$ lb, $22\frac{3}{4}$ lb, and 22 lb, apart from other big doubles including two over 19 lb.

The maximum-length paternoster that one can comfortably cast with a ten foot rod is about eight feet. This is one of the few restrictions on the tackle: that it is possible to fish an anchored bait up to eight feet off the bottom. Of course, this is quite sufficient for most waters. There is no restriction on the depth of water fishable if the anglers wish to fish the bait near the bottom, or on the bottom. One further refinement of paternostering, apart from fishing without the float altogether, is to tie the paternoster line not to the trace swivel, but to the treble hooks themselves, a system which has the effect of holding the bait very fixedly in one position. The pike do not seem to mind at all, and I have used this technique with success particularly with excessively 'Houdini-like' rudd baits.

A modification of the basic float rig defined here is to fish it well over-depth, that is lying on without paternoster. This is a modification of ledgered livebaiting and is useful to hold a bait hard on the bottom and yet keep the line clear of snags. We used this arrangement with great success, taking pike to 15 lb on a swim in the Great Ouse which has a sharp ridge, between angler and pike, upon which are zebra mussel beds with shells like razor blades. A sunken float technique can also be used with success (Fig. 16).

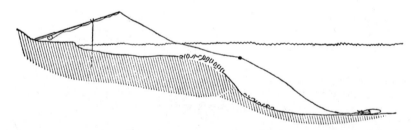

Fig. 16. A sunken float rig to avoid snaggy margins.

So far I have covered fishing almost all depths using the same basic rig, and fishing it either anchored or free-moving under circumstances where the angler considers float tackle to be better than free-lined or ledgered livebait. If it is necessary to fish shallow over deep water, say thirty feet, and yet keep the bait in one place, then I have not much advice to offer. If the water is still then the previously described outfit is perfectly adequate, but if strong drift or currents obtain then I have no practical experience of what to do. It is not a very common situation, in practice, and the only approach I have made is to actually drift or trot the bait along. It might be possible to coil up a long enough paternoster line and loosely tie the coil with that plastic-like stuff that dissolves quickly in water—the name of it escapes me.

Using exactly the same livebait rig that we are considering it is possible to switch over to static deadbaiting merely by over-deepening, and setting the two small trebles in the mackerel, herring or other deadbait. Other aspects of this technique are described in Chapters 9 and 12. Changing over to spinning or wobbled deadbaiting is merely done in the usual manner: the float, bead, and snap tackle are slipped off quickly and the appropriate traces, lures or hook mounts added: nothing new in that one.

The snap tackle described is not really suitable for very large baits, say something of the order of a pound in weight, but as far as big baits for pike are concerned I think that like Ray I am an in-between man. Discussing it once with Dave Cumpstone we decided that when we get round to fishing the hundred foot plus depths of Lough Ree we would use bream around 1 lb to 1½ lb in weight. It is just a feeling we have that not only would bream be nice and lively at depth, unlike many fish, but they would also present a bulky bait for the giant pike we feel are in the water. Both my wife and I have had a number of pike on smaller pike, but we have always had difficulty keeping the bait alive and getting it to work well. How on earth does one set the hooks in pike of 3–5 lb in weight? How can one be sure of connecting on the strike? How long does one leave a take before striking? My own feeling, shared by Dave, is that a bream of 1–1½ lb is much more likely to succeed on all counts with giant pike. But I have not had a pike of 39 lb: and the only run I ever got on a 1½ lb bream resulted in a pike of 4 lb! Big baits certainly *attract* small pike even if they finally ignore them as a rule.

As far as hook arrangements go, for what I suppose I shall have to call medium large livebaits (½ lb–¾ lb), I certainly think the Dave Steuart rigs are superb. For stationary deadbaiting I have considerable reservations about the Steuart rigs, excellent hookers though they are once a run is obtained. The Dave Steuart rig for larger livebaits consists, as all his hook rigs do, of small trebles. One is set near the dorsal fin of the bait in the usual manner, but from the shank of this treble hook project *two* short traces each terminating in a further small treble: one is set in a pectoral fin of the bait, and the other near an anal fin root. For larger bait still, the system can be extended and further hooks used even if hanging quite loose. For small pike livebaits (as opposed to fish of 3–5 lb which I have never used and probably never will) I have never been in favour of multihook rigs since the pike livebait does not seem to last very long.

This business of different types of hook arrangements stems partly from the fact that most anglers have mixed sizes of livebaits to contend with, livebait not being the easiest thing in the world to come by, and partly because to be restricted to one size of livebait would seriously affect the piker's long-term chances.

I have a dream. It occurs at regular intervals throughout the pike season. In it there is a one foot diameter grey steel pipe with a door on the end. I open the door and out comes an unending supply of six ounce 'slimies', straight into my livebait bucket. Until this becomes reality I have to make do with anything that comes along including Tommy Ruffe and tiny bleak. Once, on the Great Ouse, I had a 6-pound pike on a small carp livebait. An hour later a 15-pounder took a ¾ lb jack livebait: each success making me feel that at last I am beginning to get the hang of using small pike as livebaits. The hooking arrangement used was that of an ordinary large snap tackle. One treble was placed in the thick root of the anterior end of the dorsal fin, and the leading treble nicked lightly under the skin about half-way between the head and the dorsal fin. When livebaiting with pike as bait it is almost impossible to detect the beginning of the bite! Only after a few moments do you realize that your bait is becoming immensely powerful. And I am convinced that hooking the taking pike will always be a problem. In the case of the 15-pounder I had to strike for the simple reason that only four turns of line were left on the spool. The fish was played to the net where it was found that the ¾ lb jack had been swallowed, only its tail protruding from the big pike's throat, but the trebles were nicely positioned in the front of the lower jaw! Coupled with that the trace snapped as the fish hit the net, the hooks fell out, and my line was in the most phenomenal tangle. The reel was borrowed from Ken Powley and had a manual pickup and no slipping clutch! All in all a rather fluky capture, made less embarrassing by the fact that I had been extremely unlucky earlier in the day to get snapped by another pike—a case of overnight weakening of a monofil line causing me to temporarily abandon that reel. This business of monofil deterioration is extremely annoying; I had tested this line on the Friday, played several pike up to over ten pounds on the Saturday, and yet on Sunday the line parted at a strain of 4-5 lbs.

I think it will be clear from the foregoing that I intend my tackle to be versatile: I want to be able to fish static deadbaits or anchored or moving livebaits for variable periods, and to be able to change from one to the other quickly. I have never been one for testing a single technique to extinction! Indeed the actions of some anglers fishing for other species, usually carp, who have put in thousands of hours without a run, amaze me. Surely there is a lack of activeness of mind, or of active effort? In spite of all the preparedness outlined above I shall finish this part of the chapter by relating some incidents for which one cannot plan, and into which livebaiting can lead the piker.

When fishing a Norfolk river Bill Chillingsworth was known to turn round and say to Laurie Manns, 'Do you know, Laurie, a damned cormorant took my dace livebait yesterday!' Laurie smiled knowingly, fully aware that Bill had been on the bottle the night before. As they stood and gazed at the floats, motionless under a bright sun, the black vulture-like shape of an approaching cormorant was seen navigating seawards along the river course. As it passed Bill's float it hesitated fractionally, plopped to the water, dived, and came up smirking with Bill's dace in its beak. Poor old Bill did not even get a chance to mutter a gentlemanly 'Dearie me', as is his usual wont, but as he picked up the rod to knock hell out of the bird it dropped the dace and flew off in convulsions of mirth. Neither angler said a word, but Laurie was seen smiling faintly into a beer jug for several days afterwards. One weekend later Laurie hooked and landed a 2 lb cormorant on a 4 oz dace: it gave a spectacular fight, as good as a 4-5 lb pike, and spent the whole time under water being landed in the normal way with a net. It was very lightly hooked in the lower mandible and, after being unhooked and biting me skilfully on the arm, swam off under water at great speed. A short time afterwards it was feeding happily, just out of range of the floats fortunately.

Pike also do some weird tricks with live and deadbaits. Laurie and I were once laying on dead and livebaits on a large still water, when one of my floats rose gently in the water suggesting the bait had been picked up some fifteen feet below. A few minutes later Laurie suddenly roared, 'A damn great 20-pound pike has taken your float!' And it had. The spray was still flying as I leapt down the bank followed by Laurie and the big net. The float had rapidly disappeared and the line zipped across the water with a big shape at the head of it. I did not strike but gently pulled, and ever so gently played the fish in. Laurie crept under the fish with the net and heaved it out. Exactly twenty pounds it was, and the full story seemed to be that it had taken the bait on the bottom (for it fell out of its mouth when the pike hit the net), and then drifted up to the surface, fifteen feet up, when it rapidly got entangled in the line near the float. This strange happening occurred three times to us in one week, once more to me, and once to Basil Chilvers. Although on these occasions the float was not taken the big pike took the ledgered baits and then rose like balloons to the surface, presumably intent on swallowing it there. I can only think that the pike were feeding at the surface at the time and spotted, or smelt, the bait on the bottom below them. But clearly there is a great deal that we do not understand about livebaiting techniques because, to be honest, I do not really believe the logical idea of my previous sentence!

II

My own conversion to sliding floats for pike occurred about six summers ago when fishing Lough Allen. To attach the traditional float, a wooden-stemmed job which took bored corks in sufficient numbers to meet the demands, a loop of monofil was taken through the bottom ring (specially constructed of soft, thick plaited terylene to avoid any danger of cutting) up over the stem and back down the other side finally pulling tight on to the terylene. To adjust the depth a quick push with the line above and below the float was enough to loosen the knot and all in all I felt quite confident in the adaptability and safety of the arrangement. This frame of mind was somewhat shattered when on striking into a fish the line parted at the float. Such things happen inexplicably from time to time of course, but when the story was repeated again shortly afterwards, the break again occurring at the float, this was just too much of a coincidence. There had to be a reason and everything pointed to the knot. Back on dry land the tackle was attached to a post by digging the treble hook firmly into the wood. A length of line was run out and, after tightening up hard, a series of extremely firm strikes were made. It did not take many strikes before a break occurred and checking up I was no longer surprised to find that the line had gone at the float once again. Reverting to my former method of attachment, by which the line is not looped but taken singly three times through the float ring, the problem was solved. At this stage however, my confidence in the float's ability to take monofil without damaging it had gone, and thinking it all over, I decided that a slider was the answer. I incorporated a stop knot of cotton thread and by this arrangement the line went direct all the way to the trace swivel without any possibility of weakening and any adjustment of depth could be carried out quicker and more easily into the bargain. Previous to this incident I had always considered sliding pike floats as specialized items only to be used when fishing at greater depths than could be cast with ease, but having given them a trial I have used them exclusively for both live and deadbaiting. Not having any floats designed especially for the job in my basket at the time the central stem of one of those professionally made plastic pike floats in red and white halves was removed, the bore being just the right size for a slider once a small bead was run up the line. When I get five minutes I shall make up a number of cork floats with a biro refill-lined hole and paint them light yellow. This I think is the best all-round colour for most of the water that I fish. This business of testing the tackle strength on dry land by pulling against an immovable object is a sound idea anytime there is doubt creeping into the angler's mind about its condition. If a snag has just been, cleared, or if cigarette ash has been flung uncomfortably close, it is far better to discover the weakening these might have caused than to have a large pike find it for you.

I often used to use an adhesive on trace wire knots myself but no longer do so because I found it completely unnecessary. For

Alasticum single strand, once through the swivel eye and then twisted back around the main length for a couple of inches and you will have a secure non-slip hold, provided the turns are made at a considerable angle—90° or so. For cabled wire turn back the end couple of inches, push the resultant loop through the swivel eye, double both ends back through the loop, pull tight and finish off by twisting the shorter end round the main wire length. In this case the angle is of no importance; the knot itself provides all the holding power necessary (Fig. 17).

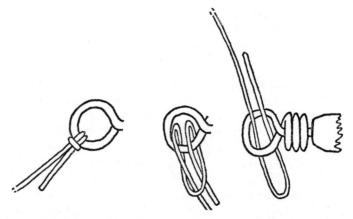

Fig. 17. Alternative cabled Alasticum knot to that depicted in Fig. 11A. Shown completed prior to twisting for approximately half an inch.

Of all the species I ever tried for livebait, and there are not many I have not tested, rudd are about as good as any from the durability point of view. They work on and on indefinitely and are also the easiest to store. I often keep half a dozen baits for the day or even several days in an old plastic dustbin outside my garage. The water has to be changed every few hours to keep roach, bream, and dace alive but with rudd twice as many baits could be left unattended for weeks. No other species could I ever find that was so convenient to store in this respect; it solved admirably one of the livebaiter's major problems.

The one instance I personally experienced of pike taking a float happened on Martin's Delph, a drain off the Witham, several years ago. Float-ledgering a herring one cold and rainy winter's day, all hope of action had just about gone when up came a double-figure pike which calmly grabbed hold of my 8 in porcupine and set off with it at a steady pace. No happy ending to this story however; I was fishing alone and the pike let go well before any chance of landing it occurred. This was not a case of taking the bait on the bottom then rising in the water to become entangled with the line. The herring was in fact completely ignored in favour of a tasteless, unsavoury porcupine quill. As an almost exclusively winter pike angler till recent summers, my experience of pike scooping a bait off the surface is limited and I can only remember one other case. That was on a pond near Grantham where I was drifting along in the old boat. A sizeable pike neatly removed a dead roach floating on the surface for all the world like a carp taking a crust of bread. It was all done so quietly that had I not been actually watching the roach at the time the incident would have passed unnoticed. Thinking back however, this was a close season trip of exploration in late April with the water temperature rapidly rising towards its summer level. Surface feeding would perhaps have been expected; fish generally tending to rise towards the surface as the warmer weather approaches. Certainly pike feed regularly just below the surface through the summer and early autumn, as I know from my own personal experience, and Fred Wagstaffe does extremely well with small surface lures in hot calm conditions. In winter such occurrences can be classed as freak behaviour however. I remember Dennis Pye writing once that of all the dead roach he had seen floating along on the surface of the Upper Thurne waters, and with salt infiltration on high tides, crop spraying and so on, the number ran into many thousands— he had never once seen a pike take the slightest notice of them as they drifted away.

CHAPTER 6

ARTIFICIALS

Ray Webb

In the nineteen-thirties spinning for pike saw a boom in popularity
in this country such as has never been seen since. I well remember
an old uncle of mine, a really ardent artificials' man sadly regret-
ting their passing out of fashion, as the trend swung rapidly in
favour of livebaiting. Largely responsible for the spinning
vogue was the tremendous success enjoyed on Hickling Broad
and the adjoining waters of the Upper Thurne by the top man of
the day, Jim Vincent. His catches were largely made on a narrow,
five-inch silver-plated spoon, a model which was eventually
put on the market bearing his name. With over twenty pike
topping the twenty pound mark to his credit, Jim Vincent failed
like so many more to land a 30-pounder, his biggest fish
falling a mere 8 oz short of this. About this time too, over in
Ireland, the angling world was well and truly rocked by the
capture of a 53 lb pike from Lough Conn by John Garvin. This
fish was taken on a silver spoon of a pattern some half the length
to that preferred by Jim Vincent.

By 1950 with Dennis Pye now firmly established on the angling
scene, spoons, plugs and the like were quickly forgotten as a
dumb-bell float, snap tackle and a 6 oz roach became very
much the done thing. Working his baits along the fringes of
the marginal reed beds Dennis's returns read like something
out of an angler's dream; 240 over 20 lb by 1963, and spectacular catches being recorded season after season. With such
astonishing results coming consistently to an intelligently
worked livebait it was hardly surprising that spinning went
out of fashion when really big pike were being sought in
earnest. The method became generally looked upon as good
fun, extremely sporting, but suitable, generally speaking, only
for the man who wanted an enjoyable day at the waterside

and who was content to fish for the smaller specimens only.

To push the use of artificials even further into the background, by 1960 the ledgered deadbait was becoming even more widely employed throughout the country, its devotees claiming with some justification that the average size taken by this method was even bigger than that obtained on livebait. Generally looked on as slow work, but effective for the really outsize pike, specimen hunters took to the new technique like a duck takes to water, and 20-pounders started to appear with some regularity from areas where previously their presence had never been suspected. It was not always slow work either. There was a considerable number of times and places where not only bigger fish but more runs were recorded by this method than to livebait. It was hardly surprising then that between them these two techniques completely dominated the pike-fishing scene.

Another decade has started however and with it come very definite signs that the use of artificials is about to come back into the picture and re-establish itself as a method to be reckoned with. With every year seeing more and more English anglers turning their attentions from our overcrowded fisheries to the lightly or even completely unfished waters of Ireland, spinning was bound to be rediscovered sooner or later: as one chap summed it up 'We used to understand artificials and how to use them, it is just that for the moment we seem to have forgotten'. Leading the way back are men like Fred J. Taylor of Aylesbury, the man who brought the herring into fashion and is now attempting to do the same for the spoon; Bill Keal, well-known contributor to *Angler's Mail* and all round big fish enthusiast; Thurlow Craig, for years a lone voice crying in the wilderness who now finds he is being backed up by very distinguished company indeed, and Fred Wagstaffe of Northampton the most ardent spinning enthusiast of all. This last man is really a treat to listen to when expounding his views on the correct use of artificials and his fervour is infectious in the extreme. To convert me he just had to be a persuasive talker, for I was exceedingly loath to even consider the method, but having made a start I am rapidly becoming ever more enthusiastic. It opens up a whole new field of piking that previously I had hardly realized existed.

One of the great problems confronting the angler when trolling is that of getting the bait down to and holding steady at whatever depth he decides to fish. Controlled to a large degree by the speed at which the boat is travelling it is extremely difficult at times, especially in rough squally weather, to keep the pace constant, the bait then rising and falling in the water in accordance with the variations. Also involved are the thickness, type and length of the line played out, the presence and positioning of any lead weights that may be incorporated and the bait itself of course: a quick change to a lure of another pattern can, and so often does, mean another series of test runs to ascertain the new working depth. If the depth of the water fished is fairly constant then fishing is comparatively straightforward, but problems arise when the bottom shelves rapidly as happens at so many points on the larger Irish lakes. When the position of rapidly shallowing water is known then the boat speed can be stepped up or the rod tip lifted to allow for it, but when, as so often happens, one is taken by surprise then heavy losses of tackle can be expected. To do the job properly an echo sounder is absolutely indispensable, advance warning of approaching shallows being given every time, or one can position the boat on a set depth contour and stay with it hour after hour. In some cases there may not be as many pike covered by this latter procedure as when a stretch of water of varying depth is fished but there will as a rule be enough fish encountered to show a worthwhile return. For one thing, time lost trying to free snagged lures, and retackling when one fails, is eliminated and the financial loss avoided can assist in maintaining solvency too. If a bait does foul the bottom, then whether it is successfully retrieved or not a thorough check for cuts and fraying on the line should be carried out for a considerable distance back from the end: further trouble awaits the angler who neglects to carry out this very necessary precaution. With certain patterns of lures the weight needed to hold them down to say twenty feet, can be really excessive. I remember Fred Wagstaffe coming in from Lough Allen one day somewhat disgusted at having to employ some 7 oz of lead! If one's pocket will run to it a modern lead-cored line will solve the problem in a more satisfactory fashion but not everyone, myself included, would be prepared to fork out for one, especially when snaggy water is being fished, where even with an echo sounder one has to expect tackle losses from time to time. Fortunately there is another more economical answer that was explained to me by Fred J. Taylor, an idea he had just brought back, as I had already suspected, from that most progressive of all countries, the United States. Lowered from the stem of the boat on the end of a stout cord is a compact solid weight of 7 lbs or so (Fig. 18). A suitably shaped rock would do for instance, and at whatever

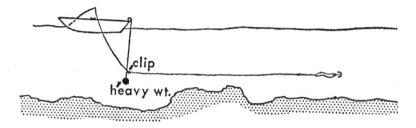

Fig. 18. Method of trolling a spinner at a set depth using a heavy weight and quick release clip (see text). Not to scale.

depth the lure is to be fished, some sort of quick release device is attached. A crocodile clip with the jaws sheathed in rubber can be used for this item, or a short length of soft metal just capable of resisting the pressure exerted by the lure; the weightless monofil being played out to whatever length is required, then attached to the quick release gadget and the weight lowered down into the water. Fixing the rod firmly in position the line is reeled in until the rod tip takes on a fair bend, a take being signified by the rod straightening up rapidly much after the fashion of a slack-line bite when tight-line ledgering a fast river for chub. When I next wish to troll a buoyant type of bait at some considerable depth this is the method I shall use. From the first moment that Fred outlined the details I became an enthusiastic convert, what with lumps of rock, bits of string and so on, the price, as I put it at the time, is very definitely right.

It is not always necessary however, or even desirable to present the lure well down even when fishing water of considerable depth. On Lough Ree for example, many of the local pike men including the top angler himself, Harry Waterstone, regularly fish a bait on completely weightless tackle when trolling twelve to fifteen feet of water and the results obtained are all the justification of the method that anyone could ever ask for. It would seem that in the clear water the pike will come up many feet to intercept a rapidly moving bait without any hesitation: either that or they are already up living and feeding in the surface layers which is quite a likely possibility in the warmer months of summer when the Irish piking season is at its height.

In addition to the working depth, the colour scheme of the lure also has to be taken into consideration. An oft-repeated maxim heard wherever one goes in Ireland (even the youngsters and the non-anglers, if any, all seem familiar with it), is the old gag about a bright bait for a dull day and a dull bait for a bright day. Somewhat overworked and of extremely distant origin though the phrase may be, the principle is sound and remains well worth serious consideration even to this day. Not only the type of day comes into it but also the time of day, at dawn and dusk a bait of a striking colour scheme will regularly take pike, the more soberly hued patterns coming into their own around the midday hours. A fair splash of yellow on a bait seems well worth a trial, the Yellow Belly and Baby Piky being two consistent killers that incorporate this colour in some profusion.

One point I have serious doubts about is the effectiveness of bar spoons with blades that actually do spin as opposed to spoons that merely wobble. When big pike of ten pounds or more are being sought there just does not seem to be any comparison. For small jack pike I know the spinning lures can be highly successful, but most of the best baits for the bigger fish are of the non-revolving variety. On the broads, Jim Vincent swore by a 5 in silver-plated wobbling type of spoon, whilst over on the Irish Loughs the traditional killer has always been a large copper and silver spoon that steadfastly refuses to spin. Over recent seasons the Abu 'Toby' has come to the fore somewhat and this again is a Jim Vincent type bait. Plug fishing is rarely practised seriously for big pike in my experience, but what little is done tends to convince me that it is more likely to succeed than spinning. Ernie Merritt takes tremendous bags of good pike from Hornsea in summer on plug. His best return for a single day was a remarkable haul of forty-nine fish. On Coosan Lough three summers ago George Higgins took a 27-pounder at the first time of offering on plug after a spoon had been refused. This was a case of a large pike sunning itself in clear shallow water. Its every move could clearly be seen and there is no doubt of its preference for the plug. It seems to me that to deceive a big pike, the nearer one's bait resemble its natural diet, the fish, the better, and revolving bar spoons are the furthest away of all in this respect. Wobblers and plugs approach much nearer to the ideal.

Provided he is equipped with a good pair of tin snips and a drill, the angler who keeps his eyes open for bits of scrap metal, old broom handles and the like can keep himself amused throughout the close season and also cut down his running expenses as well. A full range of spoons in the three- to six-inch range in silver, brass and copper will see the angler well set up to tackle most waters in most conditions, and with a plug or two thrown in for good measure he can set out for a day's fishing confident of being able to offer the pike something to their liking unless they are completely off feed. In addition to the enjoyment derived and the saving made from constructing one's own baits there is an extra satisfaction somehow when a good fish is deceived and taken by a homemade lure. This I can vouch for personally having successfully landed my two biggest pike of 29 lb and 28¼ lb on 4 in spoons that had been cut and hammered into shape on the bankside a few hours previously. If those two fish are not enough to convince me not only of the joys but also of the efficiency of homemade artificials I would like to know what is.

Such then are some of the problems and prospects, awaiting the angler who decides to turn his attention for the first time to the use of artificials. Like all other methods, it is no magical formula that guarantees success. Employed intelligently at the right time, in the right place however it will prove a valuable addition to the pike man's armoury. It fails generally in the colder months. Dennis Pye, whose piking has largely been done in the traditional October to March period on the Broads was once quoted as saying that spinning was a waste of valuable time that could be put to better use and in his particular circumstances there is some element of truth in this. In April or May with the water temperature rapidly rising, and weed growth starting to flourish, the position changes however, a surface-running plug for instance often being the only practical way of fishing a tiny hole in the middle of a thick weed bed. Many of the smaller English pike fisheries subjected to intensive fishing throughout the winter months may well be unable to stand further attention in the summertime as well, without a sharp decline in sport setting in, but on lightly fished waters or enormous expanses like the great Irish lakes that can stand being flogged no such danger exists. As that man Wagstaffe summed it up so neatly 'It is good fishing Ray, effective fishing, capable of producing 20-pounders as regularly as they have any right to be, but over and above all not only is it good fishing it is fun fishing too.' Having finally made a start at it and experienced the pleasure and profit that can be expected as a result I can only conclude that Fred, as usual, knows what he is talking about.

II

Christine's best twenty pound plus fish came to a large spoon, so of the three of us I am the odd one out taking my best on suspended deadbait. Christine and I were trolling a 7 in Jim Vincent spoon in Fred Carter's Coosan Lock in Ireland. We had an arrangement at the time: I did the rowing and Christine held the rod. As she was pregnant at the time (and indeed produced our son a week or so later) she was supposed to hand the rod to me if she hooked a big one. You will agree no doubt that this was a splendid arrangement! Using this technique I had an 18 lb fish before lunch. Anyway there I was, rowing happily away, and slowly working down a narrow channel known at Fred's as the L-shaped bay. We were about eight feet away from thick bul-rushes, and passing near a large mooring buoy, when Christine yelled 'Fish on'. I immediately turned the bows away from the rushes and mooring rope, and pulled us to mid-channel, there dropping anchor and hoping that the pike would run away from the rushes. 'Okay, you can pass the rod over to me now,' I said, scrambling along the boat. No answer. The rod, a Farstrike, doubled up as she pulled the fish clear of the bulrushes. I repeated my request, and the response was immediate, and to the point: 'Get lost. This is no piddling 18-pounder.' And so it proved: after a terrific battle I chin gaffed the fish first time and heaved it into the boat, dropping it on Christine in the process. Weighed on shore a few minutes later it went 25¼ lb. I did not really feel like rowing any more that day.

This business that Ray mentions of pike taking plug having steadfastly refused to look at a spinner is so common in my experience that I am inclined to wonder, with Ray, if there is any point in using artificials of the barspoon type. Most of my early pike taken on artificials have been on barspoons, but during the same period I took more double-figure fish on large, jointed plugs of the floating type. I intend to do a great deal more summer piking than I have done over the last four or five years, and a switch to the methods devised by Ernest Merritt and Fred Wagstaffe seems inevitable. Perhaps the most attractive feature of artificials to begin with anyway, is that you do not have to catch them first: they catch you in fact. I must admit to knowing nothing at all about the colour of artificials: all my choices of colour have been unthinking, but I have been quite happy ringing the changes. I have never had much success with copper-coloured spoons, preferring either dulled or shiny silver ones. The Voblex lures I have certainly found quite deadly, and, like the Veltic barspoons, they catch other fish than pike. Veltics are usually barred with black or red, and my choice was the former colour. I shall have to think more carefully about lure colours; Fred and Bob Reynolds certainly inspire one to do so.

I have had a fair number of double-figure pike on various barspoons but like Ray I am inclined to consider plugs of various kinds, such as Rapalas, to be superior. At the moment, prior to several years when I shall be doing more 'spinning', I feel that large plugs (say up to one foot long), single and jointed, rubber eels, and large spoons will be amongst the foremost of my artificials. Having said that I do know some waters in the East and West Ridings where the best artificials seem to be mackerel spinners. These delightful, relatively heavy little spinners can be fished about one inch deep, and because of this they were highly successful in the summer in some shallow lakes exceedingly choked with silkweed. Pockets in the silkweed were about three or four feet across and five or six feet long, and in them rested mighty pike. The technique was to retrieve the mackerel spinner quickly between the pockets, and as slowly as possible actually within them. Friends of mine had several good fish up to 25 lb, but on these waters I never made ten pounds using the normally successful technique. A matter of chance I hope.

Mackerel spinners also work farther south! In exactly similar circumstances near Cambridge I flicked a one inch mackerel spinner to a spot where dozens of rudd had earlier taken to their wings. I suspected a large chub and used six pound with no wire trace. As the tiny spinner twinkled over the centre of the disturbance a mighty eruption occurred; but the fish missed! On the second cast a similar explosion so swamped everything that I was uncertain, fractionally, whether the lure had found its target—a second later I knew, because a bow wave went straight into the soft weed and round the point of land from which I fished. I hung on tightly, the Mark IV Avon doubled over and almost wrapped around the point. The fight continued with a realization that the chub was a pike, and no small one either. Considering that the water was not supposed to contain pike it was quite a turn up for the books. I eased the pike to the surface at the first opportunity, noted the mackerel spinner blade visible outside its mouth, and proceeded to lay into it a bit. When I thought it about ready, I waded out to the gravel off the point and prepared to lift it out with my left hand: it promptly shot through my legs, leaving me standing like a drunken heron whilst I rapidly untangled things. Remarkably it was still attached, and the second attempt proved a text-book scoop out with the left hand. Weighed a couple of minutes later it went 13 lb, and was clearly the Lord of the Manor in a water that has never since yielded pike

At the moment I am spinning for a couple of hours on most piking trips, and during the last few weeks have taken nothing big on spinner and several big ones on mackerel and livebaits, best 26½ lb, from the same swims at the same time. But it is winter, the water temperature is down to 35°F, and I am beginning to think that on this rod I would be better wobbling deadbaits. There are certainly considerable advances to be made in lure fishing generally. Peter Wheat, for example, the well-known Hampshire angler, has succeeded well with large flies for large pike, and I have certainly taken small pike in Yorkshire on streamer flies. However, the best lake for this approach, a shallow clay pit, quite weed-choked in summer, also yielded numerous pike to small bunches of duckweed dragged slowly along on the surface. When I get around to using a surface floating artificial mouse or watervole this is the lake I shall choose for instant success. There is a great deal of fun to be had out of fishing artificials of all kinds, and I only hope that the idea does not creep in that this is the only sporting way to go pike fishing. This will sour it as a technique. Anglers are sporting (or otherwise), *not* angling methods.

CHAPTER 7

TACKLE

Barrie Rickards

Most discourses on tackle dwell at great length on rods, slightly less so on reels, and hardly at all upon other items of gear except hooks: most tackle catalogues list rods first, with profuse illustrations, then reels, and finally the rest of the paraphernalia of the sport. I intend in this chapter to reverse the proportion of time allotted, for a variety of reasons. In the first place many of the 'lesser' items are extremely important, probably more so than the rod, for example. I'd rather have a good landing net and a poor rod than the other way round. This is a personal viewpoint, and there are historical reasons for it, but I must say that in fitting out a newcomer to pike fishing, I'd consider the rod last of all. In order to dismiss rods I shall mention them briefly here!

In my student days I used so-called Boy's Rods sold by Tom Watsons of Nottingham for 19 shillings each. They had whole cane middle and butt sections, a lancewood top, a length of 9 feet, and a fly fisher's rod handle. I lengthened the handles myself and took quite a number of double-figure pike on them: recently I renovated them, gave two away to deserving causes and kept the other one for sentimental reasons. I also had two homemade tank aerials of 8 feet, the only virtue that I could claim for them being that they would throw herrings well: I *landed* pike in spite of the rods, not because of them. These were finally abandoned in 1969. Mark IV carp rods are useful for free-line livebaiting, and ledgered livebaiting with small baits and leads, and also for heavy deadbaiting if the bait is chucked out by hand. They are beautiful rods to play a big pike on. But my best pike rod up to 1968 was a Davenport and Fordham 'Farstrike' carp rod. Ten feet of fibreglass that will throw a herring a reasonable distance, and play a pike beautifully. My 29 lb 10 oz fish came on this rod, and it still has the original rings, ferrules and whippings in quite perfect order after being used three days a week for several years.

The best pike rod I know at the moment is a 10 feet fibreglass stepped-up carp rod made by Olivers of Knebworth. I should think the ten members of the Cambridgeshire Pike Anglers have at least twenty of these rods. But I am sure there are plenty of other good piking rods. As I say, I am far from fussy about rods, and am probably not, therefore, the best person to advise about them. I know that if I had more time and money I'd have at least one longer rod of $10\frac{1}{2}$ to 11 feet for real distance casting, possible a Leslie Moncrieff beachcaster, and certainly I should have some shorter bait-casting and spinning rods. But all that is just dreaming.

Reels by comparison are fantastically important items. If the rod snaps during playing, a fish can still be netted without trouble: if the reels jam you'll be lucky to get a big pike anywhere near the bank. The reel situation, as with rods, is extremely healthy—a great choice of fixed spools, centrepins and multipliers exists. It really is almost impossible to go wrong so I'll just mention the reels I use: Mitchels (various); Intrepid's Supreme, Elite and Challenger; Ambassadeurs, and various centrepins. I even have a cheap Polish reel the pickup of which does not snap on viciously, but rolls on smoothly due to a neat bit of machinery inside the flier: and that reel was less than the price of a Polish breakfast if I remember rightly.

I am extremely fussy about lines, not so much the make, but the quality, breaking strain and lack of flaws. I constantly run my fingers over nylon monofil searching for kinks: fraying may indicate a grooved or cracked rod ring. I do not mind so much fish shedding the hooks during playing, nor do I mind missing on the strike, but I really hate getting snapped up. The first two 'happenings' can occur through no fault of your own, but to get snapped up means there's only one thing to blame, namely yourself. Nylon monofil is of superb quality these days: some of it could have less shine, be of better colour, and be more supple, and there is no doubt in my mind that it can go 'off' overnight, but generally there are few problems. Also available are plaited nylon, terylene and courlene lines, lead-cored lines, fly lines and so on. It hardly matters which is used provided the angler constantly watches for flaws, and regularly tests the breaking strain by, at the very least, giving it a good tug.

The breaking strains I normally employ for big pike are 9 lb–15 lb, usually 11 lb, but if a great deal of casting is done a short shock leader of up to 20–25 lb can be used. Or, if fishing amongst sunken trees one might possibly wish to go up to over 20 lb. The pike angler should never be ashamed of using strong lines to suit particular circumstances, or even his own inability. There really is no merit at all in leaving pike swimming around with hooks in their jaws, in spite of the mutterings of some writers who seem to like the idea of having 'breaking-strain records'. This sort of thing makes me wonder whether the philosophical advances of the last twenty years have actually got through to some people.

I used to fish a lot with a chap we called Sharkbait Robbo. He always used enormous baits and lines of up to 60 lb breaking strain for piking. His idea was that if he ever did latch on to a 40-pounder then it was '. . . coming out, mate, it's coming out'. He also knew that he attended his lines very poorly, and calculated that even with a bad flaw a 60 lb line could hardly fail below 20 lb b.s. Everything happened to this chap, mostly through his own doing, but I once witnessed a bizarre scene on the Market Weighton canal in East Yorkshire, where he was more or less blameless as far as I could judge.

Sharkbait was fishing the rough west bank down towards the Foulness mouth and was trotting the stream with a small livebait attached by sea hooks to a cable-like trace and hence to 60 lb b.s. line. The line did not float, and the description 'trotting the stream' does not quite fit the activity. On the east bank of this narrow canal, trotting along more or less level with Sharkbait, was young Prask, another member of a somewhat fiendish specimen group. Prask got a run on his bream livebait, fished to 8 lb b.s. line, and promptly told the world about it. Not to be outdone Sharkbait also declared a run about ten seconds later. After a while it became clear that Prask and Sharkbait were pulling not so much into a fish, but more against each other, and when a fish surfaced in the middle of the canal it was downright obvious that the pike had taken both their livebaits. With loud roars, the modern equivalent of which would be 'Get knotted, Prask,' Robbo proceeded to heave with all his might towards the west bank, and Prask proceeded to heave with all his might towards the east bank. Those of us watching, quite apart from trying to contain ourselves on the bank, placed our bets on Prask for we knew the age of the 60 lb b.s. line. We won our bets, and our bank (for the rest of us were on the east bank) gained a huge float and some huge hooks, as well as a somewhat bewildered 5 lb pike. I do not think there are any morals to be culled from that episode.

If I have to put things in order of merit then, sound reels and good lines come before rods. It's nice if the rods are good too, since it adds greatly to the overall enjoyment! What about the other items of tackle the complete pike angler should carry? First of all I should say that the fully equipped pike angler looks like a packhorse. I can walk about two miles with my equipment, and not much further at one go. But always I am utterly and completely determined to move if I have to. I'll break camp after two hours' fishing and walk another two miles if I feel a mistake has been made: I'll also work slowly down a stretch of river dragging the gear along behind me. This sort of approach to angling—to take everything but the kitchen sink—is the approach that drives many anglers to become spinning-only men! Usually they have all manner of high-sounding reasons for the change, but in essence one can assume that they just cannot be bothered with carrying heavy loads. Fair enough. But remember that when those anglers are talking piking, they are really talking spinning. My own argument is that when I fancy spinning I'll spin, because in my vast rucksack I have a good selection of plugs, pikers, barspoons and other weirdies. Fully equipped I have a rucksack, a rod holdall and a livebait can. The rod holdall (Plate 1.1) is a roll-up variety designed by myself and made up by Bernie Wright, the well known Littleport saddlemaker. Richard and Hugh Reynolds and Bill Chillingsworth also use the same type of holdall, in fact Mark II versions of my original design. Rian Tingay uses a commercially made roll-up bag, the main disadvantage of which is that it does not comfortably take 5 feet rod pieces, nor does it take enough rods. I am still faintly amazed that anglers have not seized upon the roll-up rod holdall idea for it is quite superior to the standard golf bag type in which rods and rod rings are commonly damaged. Every honest angler knows full well that at the end of a long, wet day the blasted rods never go easily into the traditional holdall. With the roll-up type one simply lays it open on the ground, slots the rods into the pockets, and the brolly, and the rod rests, and then rolls it up, finally securing the roll with a strap. It hardly matters if it's raining cats and dogs because on arriving home it is merely necessary to unroll it and stand it upright against the garage wall where it and its contents will dry out more efficiently than by any other method.

The plate is more or less self-explanatory, but I would emphasize that the holdall takes eight rods in rod bags, a pocketful of rod rests (say five or six), a landing net handle, and an umbrella.

But what are its particular merits for pike anglers? Now we come to the cardinal sin which I and many of my friends indulge—we take rods already made up for fishing. There's one thing I cannot stand about angling, and that is tackling up at the start of the day, and detackling at the end of it: both activities always take place in darkness and I can do without it. So I do not detackle at night, but hook the trebles into the bottom ring of the top joint, break the rod into its two halves, and then reel everything tight, with the ratchet on. The upper joint folds down neatly by the side of the lower joint. The butt and top of the upper joint are then pushed into the same pocket in the holdall, and the joints are taped together about halfway along the holdall. The last steps are to take the reel off the rod, remove the spool, and tuck the latter into the same pocket as the rod butt. Next morning all I have to do, one hour before dawn, is put the reel on the rod and it's ready for action.

But what if you want to use a different technique mate, I can almost hear you ask. Well, the tackle set-up I have used for the last few years is designed for versatility. I can change from paternostered livebait, to free-swimming livebait, to ledgered livebait, to ledgered herring, or even spinning in the twinkling of an eye. And back again if necessary. The details of this outfit are described at the beginning of the chapter on Other Livebaiting Techniques. The principle of the approach is simple: whilst I am prepared to walk miles, time after time, and whilst I am prepared to quickly change my tackle to suit circumstances, I am not prepared to tackle up rods from scratch one hour before the usual dirty wintery dawn.

Rolled up in this manner I can get four rods, an umbrella, a landing net stick, and rod rests into the holdall, the contents of each pocket being quite protected by the rolls of canvas from contact with other rods and rod rests. And, of course, in using this technique the angler can have rods made up for different purposes, rather like the continental match anglers do. My own case may be slightly different and rather more pressing than with most anglers, for I fish with my wife and my small son, even in the cold depths of winter. Obviously I have their tackle to carry as well as my own. Hugh Reynolds has no such excuses, but he finds the approach highly satisfactory.

Deadbaits are usually carried in polythene containers in my rucksack, unless they really reek, in which case I make them walk behind. What about livebait? Most of us now favour a large livebait can adapted from a tin used by plasterers to hold stuff called Febmix Admix. The remnants of any plasterers' or builders' rubbish is carefully scoured out, and the result is a can some 13 in in diameter and 14 in high. Most close seasons are spent doing the rounds of builders' yards, and in Ireland the same cans are used at garages to hold oil. If you feel like buying them they can be obtained from the Hull firm of Robbicans, although they take some persuading to make less than a dozen at a time. All these cans have a tightly-fitting lid, and a handle with a nice wooden grip. They last about two to three seasons without rusting through, and can be used as a comfortable seat if the angler is making an effort to cut down on the tackle carried.

If the walk to your fishing is a really long haul, there are two alternatives to carrying these large cans full of water. One is to half empty it, at least. This has the effect of crowding the bait, but in this state they actually oxygenate the water rather well and after a two mile walk arrive spanking fit. The second alternative is to carry the bait in a light plastic bucket, polythene bag(!) or canvas bucket, and upon arrival transfer them to a keepnet. Generally I am not in favour of keepnets for livebait since the constant lifting in and out of the water does the bait little good. It is far better to keep the bait in these large cans and change the water regularly. With the lid on the tin they sit quite quietly, and in the depths of winter it is often unnecessary to change the water at all.

When transporting livebait cans in your vehicle beware of sudden braking. Last year I tried to avoid killing a hare, and was covered in a deluge of water and large rudd that shot into the driving seat from the back of the van. I spent the next ten minutes trying to fill up the can from a ditch with only two inches of water in it. In fact it is a great help if you can stand the livebait can in a polythene bowl or polythene bag to alleviate the problem of accidental spilling.

We also use a very neat antisplash device in the cans, thus enabling them to be filled more or less up to the brim. This device consists of a perforated disc of 1 in thick foam rubber, or polystyrene, which floats on top of the water in the can (Plate 4.5) Apart from stopping splashing it has the effect of oxygenating the water. Hugh Reynolds has noticed that if when actually fishing he leaves his bait can half full with the foam rubber in place, then he has to change the water less often than is usual. Presumably the interchange of water and air in the foam causes oxygenation of the water.

The rucksack has three pockets on the outside. One is filled with sliding floats of all shapes and sizes: round ones from half an inch in diameter up to two inches, and long sliders up to nine inches long. Another contains empty line spools which are used as bite indicators, a roll-up float wallet with enough floats and tackle for tiddler snatching, a good knife for chopping herrings and a spool of 6 lb b.s. line that is used for paternostering. A word of advice about paternoster line—either keep it on a holder that could by no stretch of the imagination be used for fishing, or else make sure the spool is not attached to a reel. Christine once set a second rod up for herself and picked up a reel loaded with 5–6 lb paternoster line by mistake. Out went the sprat deadbait, and an hour later she had a lovely run which resulted in her third best pike of $21\frac{1}{4}$ lb. That ended happily, but had it been me I'd never have got the fish anywhere near the bank.

The third outside pocket in the rucksack is filled with disgorgers, artery forceps, gags, gaffs, a roll-up bag of plugs and spinners, spare hooks, trace wire, swivels, weighing bag, balances and spare line. Gaffs have never advanced in design since they were originally made for salmon fishing, and Richard Walker's idea of a V-shaped gaff is logically quite unassailable. Ordinary U-bend gaffs work quite well but pike are quite capable of swinging off them. My gaff is an emergency tool only nowadays, as I find a landing net preferable. The debate is held in Chapter 8 on landing big pike.

Spring balances, if cared for well, are quite good instruments, and I write that despite the 'knocking' they are getting from various modern writers. I use two methods of really caring for them. One is to line the top and bottom of a shallow tin with foam so that the balances are neatly trapped by the foam. The tin is actually a 'Rob Roy' shortbread biscuit tin and is about $1\frac{1}{4}$ in deep before lining. Alternatively a balance can be wrapped thickly in a very slightly oily cloth, such as an old vest. Spring balances are supposed to vary in their efficiency with the temperature, and whilst I accept this as fact, I doubt if the correction necessary is very great. What one should do regularly with spring balances is take them in to the weights and measures inspector for checking. This will be done free of charge, and if the balance *is* slightly out he will tell you exactly how much at each weight. I once had a bream in Eire that took my spring balance right down to the stop which was at 8 lb 6 oz. Subsequent testing of the balance by the inspector showed that the balance was over-weighing by 2 oz at 8 lb. So I called the bream $8\frac{1}{4}$ lb, and doubt if it could have been many ounces more.

When I broke the pike-perch record with a fish over twelve pounds in 1970, it was weighed on the bank on three spring balances belonging to myself, Basil Chilvers and Laurie Manns. On each balance the fish went fractionally over $12\frac{1}{4}$ lb. We called it 12 lb 5 oz. This is a good field test of a spring balance— if it gives the same weight on different balances you can be fairly certain that both are correct. Later on in the day the fish was weighed by Peter Tombleson of the British Record Fish Committee and the weight came in at a few drams over 12 lb 4 oz. Subsequently, however, this beam balance was found to be slightly inaccurate and the final official weight was 12 lb 5 oz! Full justification for our spring balances. The dial balances which are becoming so popular are no doubt perfectly adequate, but there are some makes in which the needle flickers so much that an accurate reading is virtually impossible. These balances are also more bulky and difficult to care for.

The rucksack itself is a waterproof variety of the traditional style, not the modern hi-pack type which is useless for anglers, and I believe mine goes under the name of 'B-B Senior'. This firm used to do a better rucksack, called the 'super-Senior' but had to discontinue it through lack of sales. Anyway you can leave these rucksacks out in a violent storm and although they will be covered in puddles not a drop will enter the interior. At the top of the rucksack, just under the flap itself I usually have a small folding seat, a foam off-cut cushion contained in half a polythene fertilizer bag, and a big keepnet also held in half a fertilizer bag. The fertilizers themselves may not do anglers much good, but the bags are useful for keeping various items separate and dry. If you get a bootful during the day you can also wear them on your feet. I haven't much time for fishing baskets mostly because they take some carrying, but also because I cannot get all my tackle into them. If a lot of walking is to be done, with a fair weight, then the number of parcels should be cut to a minimum.

The rucksack then contains the usual stuff, including quantities of food and perhaps a stove, but has one final item which may be of great value of pike anglers. This is the tin and contained trace and snap tackle holder illustrated in Plate 1.2. The balsa 'log' is derived directly in design from a Yule log that Ray used one Christmas for wrapping multihook rigs around. A couple of hardboard discs at the ends of the balsa keep the log itself away from the sides of the tin and leave enough room for the hooks between the tin and the wood. A space at one end is left to allow a small handle to be fitted to one of the discs. The dried milk tin illustrated is ideal for the job. Not only do the hooks remain untangled, and the traces unkinked, but also the hooks do not get stuck in inappropriate places. As a guide to size and shape, most anglers will remember the familiar tins of National Dried Milk issued at welfare offices. Multihook rigs, snap tackles, and traces can be held in place on the balsa log by means of mapping pins.

It will be apparent to the reader that I have not discussed, so far, certain other tackle items: landing nets, gags, forceps, and weighing bags, among others. These are dealt with specifically in Chapter 8 in direct connection with the landing of pike, and the treatment of pike once they are on the bank.

PLATE 7

So close to thirty pounds. 29 lb fish from Lough Ree taken on 4" homemade copper spoon.

PLATE 8

Sheltering in the lee of Swan Island, Horsey Mere.

II

My own feelings on pike rods are much the same as Barrie's, the difference being that any casual observer strolling along the bank behind us would see positive evidence in my case. I do in fact only possess one rod that could be said to have any pedigree at all; and that could do with a new cork handle, butt cap, a set of rod rings and re-whipping all round. About the others the least said the better, yet the pike keep on coming to the net just the same. I cannot off-hand think of a single instance of my losing a fish that could be attributed to any inadequacy of the rod in use. In piking the line and trace strength employed afford such a wide safety margin that in practice any rod that will show any sort of action curve at all while a fish is being played will do all that is required of it. The only point I do insist on is that it is not too sloppy, otherwise casting power will be lost; and the ability to drive the hooks firmly home will be missing too.

In the matter of reels for piking a fixed spool job is essential where distance casting is required but the complex design and mechanism inherent with these patterns does bring in dangers too. In the case of some of the cheaper models the spool itself is just not up to the job of playing big pike. I've seen several instances where the bakelite spool shattered under the strain, the fish making good its escape as the ensuing 'bird's nest' of line became jammed in the rod rings. One spool, on a reel from a very famous firm that shall be nameless, didn't actually disintegrate, but what did in fact happen, was that the two halves that slotted together to form the whole unit just came apart; the result of inadequate adhesive presumably, but the result was the same, another lost fish as the tangled line refused to pay out. Gear wheels too, after a season or two hard fishing, will often start to exhibit signs of wear and tear, usually slipping under the pressure exerted by a hard-fighting pike. These and other possible troubles have to be constantly watched out for when a fixed spool reel is being employed. There is a case to be made out for a good centrepin, especially for short-range fishing. The simplicity of design and rugged durability of the materials used in construction virtually guarantee trouble-free performance indefinitely. A quick rub down with a cloth and a spot of oil on the spindle from time to time are all that is required in the way of maintenance.

Realization of the unsuitability of keepnets for housing live-bait came to me when I first fished the Norfolk Broads. It took three to four hours to obtain a supply of bait but much less than that to kill them off in a keepnet hung over the side. The fifteen or twenty minutes in each swim, then up anchor and move on technique commonly employed on those waters, invariably proved fatal in double quick time. My answer to the problem, both on the Upper Thurne fisheries and Hornsea too was a red plastic dustbin fitted with a circular, double baffle plate type anti-splash lid incorporating staggered ventilation holes that proved extremely effective in practice. They were big enough to keep the water adequately oxygenated with an absolute minimum of renewal. At least I thought it was the minimum till October 1962 when a trip to Holland saw me fishing from a Dutch boat that had a built-in livebait-well-cum-seat, the sides being perforated to allow a constant flow of water as the boat was rowed along. If ever I build another boat this is one feature that will be an absolute must; this and a free-running pulley wheel at the prow to take the rope as the anchor is being lifted. I've raised blisters on my hands time and time again for want of one of these items. Anchors themselves can be something of a problem on a rocky bottom, a really firm hold is not too difficult to obtain in these circumstances but the retrieving can prove a tricky business. Taking the boat upwind and reversing the angle of pull works sometimes but not always. When the bottom is level and snag free however, such a weight is required to hold a position with a force nine gale howling along that retrieving can become well beyond the capabilities of the man out on his own. What is needed is something more in the nature of a trained tug of war team to tackle the job. Problematical though this anchoring to a position can become, the difficulties just have to be overcome or a rapidly freshening wind will see the angler being dragged away out of casting range of a shoal of pike that have just begun to feed in deadly earnest.

When it comes to terminal tackle I'd been using single-strand Alasticum for several seasons with little cause for complaint until I started using large spoon baits for casting and retrieving. In times of high winds especially, on a number of occasions, I was dismayed to see the bait and myself part company after a kink had formed in the wire trace during the cast, some quite expensive baits being lost as a result. It would seem that the play of the wind on my bulky but none too heavy spoons was allowing the line to fall slack, so giving the wire a chance to double back on itself; a problem I'd not previously encountered when using ledgered herrings, a much heavier bait that is rarely cast out anyway. A quick switch to braided multi-strand Alasticum both for spinning and livebaiting has met the situation admirably, no further trouble at all. For deadbaiting I'm still quite content with the single strand variety, as I'm sure I should be, for Bill Giles and his inseparable partner Reg Sandys have hauled out several tons of pike over the years on it without running into trouble. If it is good enough for them it will do for me I guess.

CHAPTER 8

LANDING BIG PIKE

Barrie Rickards

It can be really shocking to witness the manner in which some anglers come prepared to do battle with big pike. One weekend we saw a double-figure pike gaffed in the belly on a water where pike have to be returned, by byelaw. In fact, considering the number of pike killers there are around in my own district, Cambridgeshire, it is surprising that some pike anglers are hoping to get summer piking introduced into the area: at least in the depths of winter, some of the killers hibernate, and the area remains one of the best pike regions in Britain. It is an interesting aside that the rest of the fishing is also superlative.

On the same day that the pike was belly gaffed, another 'angler' dragged a fish more than half a mile along the bank to get it weighed. When taxed by Hugh Reynolds it turned out that the fellow had no balance or weighing net, no gag, no pliers, no forceps, and no disgorger. He had no idea how to unhook the pike without these implements, and was merely wandering down the bank until he found someone who could help. This angler was not unknown in the world of angling and caused us to wonder about the actual experience of some of our angling writers.

Let us start with the playing of big pike. The actual power of the fight varies so tremendously, summer and autumn pike and 'wild' pike usually fighting better than most, that it is difficult to advise a set procedure on playing. It is worth remembering that pike, having bony mouths, tend to shed the hooks more often than most fish so that the longer it is in the water the greater the chance of losing it on that score alone. If a pike manages to reach weed my own plan is to keep tugging hard using all the strength of the tackle and the weight of the pike's body to help break free. I have never yet succeeded in pulling a pike out of big sunken boulders once it has got the line under the edge of one.

Leaping pike are great fun, but an absolute menace at the same time! Again, my own scheme is to hang on tightly, and by laying the rod right over to the horizontal I then try to make it dive. Only recently I played in a poor-fighting fish of around fifteen pounds hooked on livebait, and when close to the shore it started wallowing in the waves. It simply would not dive, and came slowly at me with its mouth open all the time: the hooks shot out when it was about two feet off the waiting net. Christine once had a fish of 19½ lb on a 7 in spoon on Lough Ree that spent about eighty per cent of the battle in the air. At one point it stood on its tail, head shaking violently in the air and travelled about ten yards with its tail lashing the water like a badly set outboard motor. There was no problem in keeping the line taut on that one! Quite recently an angling writer caught an eighteen pound pike and remarked that there was not much difference between one of eighteen pounds and one of twenty pounds! On the waters I fish you can usually tell during playing whether it is, in fact, a 20-pounder as opposed to one of eighteen or less. That two pounds extra weight means that, on eleven pounds line, it is just that little bit more difficult to move the fish through the water when it momentarily stops fighting. One way to get a twenty pound plus fish on the move again, if it goes dead on you, is to give it a series of taps or little strikes.

But do you net them or gaff them once you have them close to the bank? There is no doubt that a pike properly gaffed, at the very point of the lower jaw, suffers no harm at all and I have gaffed several pike over twenty pounds both from the bank and from a boat. A twenty pound pike is a big fish, however, and it takes a strong person to lift one into the boat with his left hand whilst holding the rod in his right. I doubt if a man on his own could efficiently gaff a fish of 30 lb into the boat. From the bank the situation may be slightly easier in that once the point of the gaff has gone home, the pike may be *slid* to the bank. The number of occasions on the bank when you couldn't do this are too numerous to think about! If a friend gaffs your pike for you then he has to be a friend, make no mistake about that.

Gaffs are cheap, easy to make, and easy to carry, whilst nets of the right size are expensive and quite difficult to buy anyway. These facts alone endear many anglers to the gaff. It also gives some lesser anglers a feeling of power, and the gaff can also be used for fending off wild bulls and the like! There are several 'don'ts' to be observed when owning a gaff, apart from fending off bulls. One, is not to gaff a pike before it is lying reasonably quietly: and the longer this takes . . . you know the rest. Another good piece of advice is to try to do the whole thing in one smooth movement after the point has gone home. On the bank it is imperative to slide the fish quickly away from the edge, then slip out the gaff point, and *put the cork back on immediately*!

It is not the done thing to gaff pike under ten pounds in weight since it is really quite unnecessary. They can so easily be lifted out by hand, and anyway pike under ten pounds are friendly chappies, not opponents. What about a really giant pike, would I gaff it or net it? If my net was big enough I'd net it every time.

There you see, I've confessed. I prefer to net my pike. After years of both using nets and gaffs, I find that a big net is a gentler and surer tool. This popular idea of pike rolling up in the net and getting the hooks entangled therein, and perhaps stuck in the pike as well, really only happens with lively, jumpy, little pike, and not very commonly at that. There is not much point in netting pike that are much under ten pounds, even when the hooks are inside the pike's mouth. If the plug you are using is visible, and bristling with hooks, then a little care is needed when scooping it out with the left hand (or right hand, if you are a left-handed fisherman). I must say that I am not keen on that method of landing whereby the angler grasps the fish at the back of the head with fingers and thumb: it certainly is not a good technique with double-figure fish, and seems a bit dodgy to me even with little ones since a fair amount of pressure needs to be applied. What I do when scooping out fish is to put my left hand under the belly slightly forwards of the midpoint of the pike and lift. If the pike slips, I let go and lift again.

But double-figure pike are no problem in landing nets. Even when hooks are visible outside the pike's mouth I can never recall having much trouble with tangles, and of the hundreds of pike that I've had I cannot remember one being injured in any way. A big fat pike on hitting the net slumps to the bottom of it. Whilst strain should be taken off the net frame, the pike should not itself be lifted but the mesh above it grasped firmly and the whole lot heaved ashore and well away from the bank. If the hooks are inside its mouth the pike can then be slid out on to the grass. If the hooks are showing outside the jaws then immediately upon lowering to the ground the pike should be held firmly. This is best done by holding both the tail and head down, or even gently sitting astride it.

My own landing net has a four foot handle. Longer handles I find rather too heavy to wield effectively when fishing on my own. The diameter of the *round* frame is 29 inches. My next one will be 33 inches or thereabouts. As well as being expensive

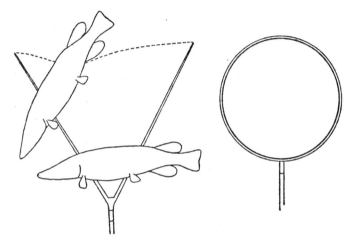

Fig. 19. Triangular landing net frame with pike in awkward positions: effective netting area is considerably reduced, and is less than the overall 'smaller' round-framed net shown on the right.

landing nets are cumbersome, particularly when the angler is roaming the banks. Some of the *very* large triangular frames are exceedingly cumbersome and exceedingly expensive, but they have the advantage that any pike in Britain could be landed in them. The average sized triangular landing net frames (usually billed as *big*) are very average tools for the job. Firstly, they have a drawstring between the extremes of the arms which gives sickeningly when a big pike stiffens across it (Fig. 19). When a big pike goes stiff you need a quarter inch thick piece of silver steel to encourage it to bend into the net, *not* a piece of cord. I must admit that triangular frames *look* the part mind you.

I had one of these stiffening pike last season. It took a tiny rudd fished about one foot away from a brick wall that ran into the water. After running deep in circles for some minutes, during which time I realized I had a 20-pounder chonking around, it came up to the top and sulked just under the surface. It refused to come right up to the top but swam quite slowly, but so powerfully round and round and round. When it stopped momentarily I couldn't move it an inch. After some minutes of this it amazed me by popping up to the top like a cork and lying there on its side. I heaved and heaved and it very very slowly slid over the net: and then it stiffened and refused to bend in. I lifted the frame slightly, exerting pressure on the region of the tail root and just behind the head, and it grudgingly bent into the vastness of the net. That one went exactly 29 lb.

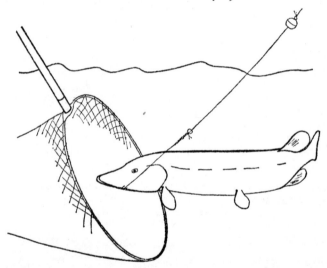

Fig. 20. Allowing a big pike to swim into a deeply sunk net.

The same fish on a triangular frame would have bent the cord, or slid off the arms (see Fig. 19). So it's a big round net for me every time. How exactly does one wield it? The old rule of sinking the net and then lifting only when the pike is over it, is very sound. It pays to watch that the mesh has not fouled a branch or rock just before lift off, otherwise you can be in trouble. There are also occasions when it is useful, with a really big fish, to tilt the net so that the fish actually swims deep into the folds (Fig. 20). Finally, one can creep up behind a pike with the net and scoop it out, an undignified approach sometimes necessary when the fish lies awkwardly in the stream and refuses to budge its angle (Fig. 21). I remember scooping a 16¾-pounder for Ray a split second after it had ejected his livebait, and the surprise and joy on his face at seeing his 'lost' fish heaved from the water really made the day. The more I think about it the more sure I am that the landing net is the more gentle, versatile and surer tool for getting pike on the bank.

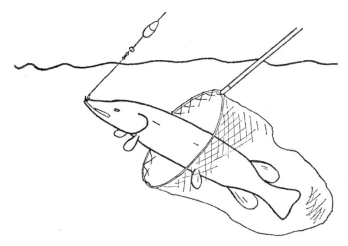

Fig. 21. 'Scooping' a pike lying awkwardly in the current.

There is just one other point to watch during playing and landing of your fish, and this is something many anglers forget about until it is too late—beware of other tackles in the area. When using ledgered baits for example it is quite easy and reasonable to use two or three rods in the one swim; or you may be sharing a hotspot with two or more friends. On getting a run the technique is to sink the other rods and lines and play in the pike over the top of them: it is amazing how quickly nylon monofil will sink. The procedure is illustrated in Plate 3.3.

The real angling farces are seen during the unhooking procedure. This varies from the one extreme where the angler stands about a yard away from his prey and prods at it hopefully with a disgorger, to the other where it is obvious that the man would be in his element in a butcher's shop.

The standard, popular, procedure is to hold the pike firmly on the ground, insert a gag into its mouth in order to open the jaws, and take out the hooks by gripping them with pliers. Long-nosed pliers are refinements, as are gags with points protected with adhesive tape. The snags are that when lying on the deck a pike is inclined, nay, strongly inclined, to leap or at least arch its back, and at the same time shake its head. The gag flies loose and whole procedure starts again. It is not a simple matter to get a protected gag into a pike's mouth, and a 20-pounder can hold closed any gag on the market, should it be so inclined. However, the system does work reasonably well even if it is a bit fiddly. It is more efficiently carried out by two anglers, one holding the trace and gag, and the other wielding disgorger and pliers. Some coordination is helpful: the man holding the trace should know when to hold it tightly and when to slacken off. If he doesn't know then the man doing the unhooking should tell him. An angler fishing on his own needs to hold the trace in his left hand and the pliers in his right. Who holds the fish?

Just recently one well-known pike angler, I think Dennis Pye, came up with a method of unhooking which involves gripping the front of the pike's lower jaw with the left hand thickly protected by a cloth. The head of the pike is lifted well off the floor, and the result is that it opens its mouth, or at least can be encouraged to do so if the top jaw is pushed a little. This method is similar to one that we in Cambridge have used for several years and both methods are far better than the traditional gag-and-pliers approach. Furthermore they are particularly useful for the lone angler.

Our method is to insert the left forefinger and second finger between the last gill raker and the gill cover; that is well clear of any gill filaments. Lift the pike (or its head and shoulders in the case of a 20-pounder) clear of the ground. The effect, again, is that the pike opens its mouth, or can easily be made to do so by pushing the upper jaw with the left thumb. Then for pike with the hooks well inside the mouth instead of using pliers and disgorger from the front, take a pair of artery forceps, close the forceps jaws so that they are quite smooth, and insert them through the gill covers keeping the forceps jaws closed all the time. Grip the hook shank, slacken slightly on the trace (held under the left thumb) and unhook by turning the hook upside down when the barb will pop neatly clear of its hold. Let go of the hook and pull it gently clear with the right hand. Close the jaws of the forceps and withdraw them carefully.

It sounds rather complicated but is easy, smooth, and safe in practice. Of course, with lip-hooked pike the forceps can be used from the front and the pike lifted as described. The frontal approach of the traditional method of unhooking makes it difficult to turn the hooks upside down which is the key to rapid unhooking of pike. For all sizes of pike and all hooking arrangements this forceps technique works better than the traditional method: five of us once neatly unhooked 102 pike in three days' fishing so the new technique cannot be bad!

At this point of having unhooked the pike it is advisable to move the hooks and rod well clear of any weighing procedures. Quickly check the trace, for this last few minutes is just the time when it gets kinked. The really dangerous kind of kink that completely ruins Alasticum wire, whether single strand or cabled, is illustrated in Fig. 11 B.C. If you get a kink of this kind then under no circumstances use the trace again, for the breaking strain will drop to about 2–3 lb on a 10 lb wire trace.

The last stage prior to returning the fish quickly to the water is the weighing. A most enjoyable part of the event usually, but things can go wrong nevertheless. If the hook of the balance is stuck in the pike's jaw and the pike lifted clear of the ground, it usually leaps: if the angler has his finger through the ring of the balance then there is a fighting chance that his finger will get broken as the pike twists. More commonly the spring balance breaks. Either grip the whole ring in your fist, or better still weigh the pike in a weighing net when nothing—pike, angler or balance—gets injured. The best weighing net material is that very soft nylon cloth which, made up with tiny curtain rings at the four corners weighs about 1 oz! Bob Benton of Cambridge Specimen Hunters showed me this system, and it improves even on polythene bags which tend to hold water and improve the weight of the pike somewhat.

The whole business from the pike hitting the net to being returned unharmed should take about two or three minutes at the most, much less in the case of small pike which do not receive the honour of being weighed. If photographs are to be taken the pike can be retained quite happily in a large, soft keepnet or open weave sack. I prefer a net, but can think of no objections to a sack. And let us hope that one day we shall see an end to the maltreatment of pike: the moral is to get fully equipped for the job before doing it, and experienced in theory before practice. A bad mistake with a big pike and it can die, and the best way to ruin a big pike water is to kill big pike as the anti-pike brigade well know.

II

In my early piking years the landing of pike, what few there were, was invariably done with a gaff unless the fish was considered small enough to be lifted out by hand. Initially some of the attempts were crude in the extreme but rapid progress in the technique was made to the point where I'd very little doubts as to whether the contacted pike would finally finish up on the bank or not. Around 1964 or '65, with 20-pounders starting to figure in my diary jottings, the gaff was still being used right up to the day mentioned by Barrie when he used his outsize landing net to scoop out a fish of mine that had shed the hooks some two or three seconds previously. I don't know which of us was the more surprised, me or the pike. No hope of landing that one could possibly have been entertained without a net and from that point on I swung rapidly away from the use of the gaff. Properly used by a man who knows how to handle such an instrument it can be quite effective, but extra time is needed to play the pike to a standstill every second of which is in the fish's favour so it's netting for me everytime these days. For a frame I use an alloy sprint rim discarded by a track cyclist, the diameter of 26 in being ample to cope with any pike I'm ever likely to hook and being alloy it is light enough to carry around without undue fatigue. For anglers who travel by bus or train it does pose something of a problem, being non-collapsible, but with one's own transport it can be strapped on to the roof rack without any trouble. A spot of netting some 3 ft deep or so plus a 5 ft handle, in alloy once again to cut down the weight, completes the outfit. One well-known writer went into print not so long ago saying that the damage done to pike by using a landing net was far greater than by any other method and if one uses 2 in mesh or more there could well be something in this statement. By going right down, as I do myself to minnow mesh the danger is cancelled out, neither fins nor anything else are likely to get entangled in this, and as I usually employ just one treble, size 2, for my pike fishing there is not much chance of trouble with the hook getting caught up either.

One technique that is employed by Bill Keal (its inventor), Fred Wagstaffe and Bob Reynolds when fishing from a boat is to use the net and frame only, a large triangular folding job with a drawstring attached, a pole being considered an unnecessary encumbrance. As one man is playing the fish to the surface the other leans over the side, opens up the arms of the net frame, sinks the pike deep into the mesh, closes the arms once again and hauls the lot aboard. My initiation to the method was something of a tense affair, for Fred was into what was obviously a good fish as he explained the drill to me, Bob being stood off in a dinghy several yards away with the camera clicking away merrily. Failure to do a good job of the netting, new though the technique was to me, would have been completely inexcusable but I need not have worried. The theory worked out fine in practice and out came the fish. That one too went 23¼ lb. Many times after that I saw the old folding frame go into action, a really effective method indeed; it's a pity it cannot be worked by the man fishing on his own as well.

From the playing angle I too have experienced many variations in fighting power of pike. The old salmon man's grouch that 'It came in like a log, old chap—literally no more fight in it than that,' can I'm afraid so often be true especially with the bigger fish around the 20 lb mark. Many factors could well be involved in this; the strength of tackle used; the type and size of the bait; the time of year; the depth, clarity and above all perhaps the temperature of the water. Fish that tend to go in for aerobatics are beyond all shadow of doubt largely affected by temperature, being quite common on a number of waters through the summer months, right up to around the end of October. Once the water really starts to cool down they become so rare that the possibility can be just about ruled out altogether. Salmon of course have a considerable push of water to boost up their fighting powers and having taken a number of big pike from fast streamy swims I can vouch for the scrap they put up in these circumstances. One can be grateful for the rest afforded by the unhooking and weighing procedures after a ten minute all out tug-of-war believe me. It is from the still waters in the depths of winter that the sluggish pike are regularly encountered and I would not attempt to minimize their failings here, a spiritless swirl or two as they are brought to the surface being often all that is offered in the way of a fight. Personally when the weight involved is obviously around 20 lb mark I've no objection to raise. These are the fish I want on the bank as quickly as possible to cut down the risk of the hooks pulling out. I am happy to settle for really hard sporting battles with the 10-pounders or thereabouts; a lost fish in that sort of weight range not being a dreadful shock. Fortunately for me this is so often the way it works out in practice, a 10-pounder regularly providing all the speed, strength and stamina that any angler could wish for. One of the most unusual performances in the way of a fight came from Barrie's first 20-pounder taken on ledgered livebait fished close into the bank. On tightening up to strike the hooks home it was found that the pike had come even closer in still, being now literally right under the rod tip some eight feet or so down. That is where it stayed throughout the encounter neither taking out line or moving to right or left, just a steady downwards pull all the time. Finally brought to the surface and netted that one went 23¾ lb, a really short solid fish of a mere 38 in in length.

CHAPTER 9

TACKLE AND TECHNIQUES: FIVE YEARS ON

Barrie Rickards

The tackle, techniques and approach to piking that we outlined in the first edition has certainly caught on in the intervening period if we are to judge by the letters received and anglers we have met. Things have changed, of course, and it is my hope to describe some of those changes in this new chapter, and perhaps give a pointer or two to the future of pike angling. In the introductory chapter to the first edition we wrote, towards the end, 'It is our dream that a modern generation of pike anglers will arrive . . . '. They have. And it is now commonplace to see on the banks far greater skill than either Ray or myself can employ, and a much greater clarity of thought being applied to piking than either of us can achieve. The mental effort of getting things right for the book has also improved our own game and my totals at the time of writing (July 10th 1975) stand at 527 double-figure fish and 36 twenty-pounders.

But on the subject of catches one other thing happened to me in this intervening period, namely that after catching big pike of 28 lb, 29 lb, and 29 lb 10 oz I finally got one of over thirty pounds, 31½ lb to be exact. (See Plate 13). It happened like this.

Laurie Manns and I had arrived before dawn on one of our favourite Norfolk waters, on November 5th to be precise. I tackled up before light with a mackerel tail on one rod, a mackerel head on another and a livebait tackle on a third. I wouldn't use the third rod until I could really see what I was doing: all had 1½ inch diameter sliding floats, a small homemade snap tackle, and 12 lb b.s. Super Maxima monofil line. Both deadbaits were cast out about forty yards in the same swim. As soon as it got light I flicked out the livebait gear with a 2 oz rudd bait, and was rewarded at 6.30 a.m. with an indignant pike of 1½ lb. It was whilst I was recasting this tackle that I saw my mackerel head tackle drift out of position. Nothing further happened and I put it down to a quirk of surface drift. Actually it was a bit of a nuisance for to make the cast in the first place I'd had to wade out into thick reed beds with the water lapping close to the top of my waders. Now I had to recast, and I made a real pig's ear of it; the line turning the farthermost reed-beds into something approaching a wickerwork basket. Eventually I got everything free again, checked for kinks, and then made a lovely 50 yard cast to exactly the spot I wanted.

Laurie and I settled back in our chairs, and we didn't get a run for 5 hours! We tried pretty hard, covering the water, leaving baits static, drifting them, and so on, but all to no avail until my mackerel head tackle (which I hadn't moved at all because of the difficulty of recasting) started to move away from the bank. This time there was no doubt about it and a fairly fast run developed. I struck when the run had gone twenty yards, though this only took a few seconds, but before swinging the rod back over my head I had the forethought to move along the bank to a clear space, holding the rod high to lift the line clear of the reeds. My strike met with a *very* solid thump and head shake at a distance of some 70 yards, and the fish then took off to my right at consider-able speed. I let it go, for it was running away from the big reed bed. It then turned on its heel and came at me from 80 yards out and travelling at a great lick. I had some difficulty keeping up with it but finally made violent contact about three yards out from my feet. Laurie was already there with the net as the great fish came to the surface just out of reach. It opened its mouth, shook its head, and the mackerel head bait was fired for several yards with considerable force. For a split second I thought the hooks were still in the mackerel, but I soon learnt otherwise as the fish tail-walked for five yards with its whole body quite vertical and airborne. The rod was pulled savagely over as the fish hit the deck again, and with no chance for me to get the upper hand the pike, obviously a 20-pounder, travelled fast into the reed bed, turned parallel to the bank, got some twenty yards of reeds between it and me, and then turned out into open water! At that point I thought I'd had it, for the sight of twenty yards of reeds bending like a swathe of corn towards the open water, convinced me that the line would be sliced through any second. But it wasn't, and the big fish stayed in the open water, making several deep and powerful runs, before

PLATE 9

After years of missing by ounces, Barrie's first twenty pounder weighed
in at $23\frac{1}{4}$ lb. Technique: ledgered livebait.

PLATE 10

Martin Gay with a 30¼ pounder taken from a Kent lake.

popping to the surface a second time, only this time within reach of Laurie's casually wielded net. I was convinced it was another 29-pounder, but all the spring balances showed it well over 30 lb, and when the weight and measures people checked these instruments the weight was pronounced at 31½ lb. It was a superb fish, as you can see from the plate. And it probably still swims for it was quite unaffected by its capture and was a young fish.

The static deadbait used, the head end of a mackerel, is of interest because only the week before the capture I had been told that the head end wasn't much use for deadbaiting. That 30-pounder was my fourth or fifth over 20 lb on the head end, not to mention numbers of double-figure fish. Of course the tail end looks much better, though it is not much more aerodynamic, and I think anglers are influenced by the former factor. I still feel that the mackerel is a better deadbait on most waters than herrings, although I have fished one water with Martin Gay where herrings are quite definitely preferred to mackerel. One of the more pleasant changes in piking during the last few years has been the willingness of anglers to experiment with different types of deadbaits: sardines, sprats, mullet, and, more commonly nowadays, freshly killed roach, dace and so on.

Under no circumstances could one consider Ray's deadbaits freshly killed but John McAngus and myself have both achieved considerable success using roach and dace hard on the bottom. I'm not convinced that in general they are much better than herrings, but like mackerel tails they can be cast a long, long way, and on many gravel pits that can be a terrific advantage.

One of the things quite new to many anglers five years ago was the technique of suspending a deadbait off the bottom, or indeed, the use of a slightly buoyant bait fairly close to the bottom. The latter effect can be achieved quite simply by using a roach or dace with an intact swim bladder, and then placing a swan shot at a variable distance from the tail of the bait: the variable distance, and current strength, dictates the distance above the bottom that the bait will float. Or air can be injected into a mackerel or herring by using a syringe. This last trick is a great improvement on the method we described in the first edition whereby a piece of balsa or polystyrene is stuffed down the throat of the mackerel: what do you do when you want the deadbait to stand on its head? The mind boggles. The only trouble with syringes is that you must get one with an aperture of 1 mm or greater, otherwise it is extremely difficult to inject air into the stiff flesh. The amount of air can be closely controlled so that the bait sinks extremely slowly and settles like a feather on the tenderest weed shoot, or actually floats up above an anchoring lead. I am certain that on some waters anyway a featherlight deadbait is taken with more confidence. Suspended sprats may well prove to be one of the successful methods of the future. I have used the system rather more than usual this last winter, using ordinary livebait gear but with a large single hook, and took a surprising number of good fish on it. I rather feel that the smell from suspended sprat homes in on the pike more quickly than it does from a sprat lying hard on the bottom. All this success is due to the advice of a friend who shall, for the present, remain nameless. By varying the amount of paternoster lead a variable drag or drift is possible using the wind drift or current.

Talking about static, buoyant and drifted deadbaits leads me naturally on to the subject of wobbled deadbaits. There is no doubt as to the success of this method in the summer months, where I rate it second only to livebaiting. But in winter the wobble has to be slowed down to an occasional twitch for the effectiveness to be maintained: the normal summer retrieve, taking only a minute or two, is often just too fast for winter pike. Even so I'd put the method pretty well down the list of successful winter baits which reads: livebait, static deadbait, twitched deadbait, mobile (wobbled) deadbait, spun deadbait, spinners etc. in that order.

The actual baits used can be quite variable but freshly killed roach and dace take some beating, followed by sprats perhaps. The last are not very tough. Jim Gibbinson showed years ago that hard, preserved baits (preserved in formalin, that is) were very effective and whilst the smell put off the angler the pike wasn't too worried. Today, of course, we build up a stock of deep-frozen baits.

It is quite possible to fish the ordinary small hook snap tackle with wobbled deadbaits, but the rig devised many years ago by Fred J. Taylor is certainly much better: this consists of threading the trace from the vent through the mouth and pulling a *large* treble into the region of the vent. The treble shank should be stopped from sinking too deeply into the bait by means of a large shot, piece of polythene etc.

Although the take on wobbled baits can be just as variable as with any other technique, my experience is that gentler bites are more common. Naturally you are feeling carefully during the retrieve and the slightest doubtful pluck should be treated as a take. Do *not* strike violently at this point, a natural temptation when just starting the sport, but take off the pick-up, or pay out line, and from that moment treat the take as you would a livebait or static deadbait run. One of the very first times I tried wobbled sprat I struck savagely at the first four takes, all from good pike on the Barmston Drain that I had spotted before casting to them, and each time I failed to connect. Nowadays I wait until the line is ticking off slowly before I tighten up and belt it one.

Having denigrated the wobbled deadbait just a little, it should be added that there are times in the depths of winter where, just as with suspended deadbaits, it is preferred by the pike to livebaits in the same swim. There can be no doubt whatsoever that the pike know the bait is dead, so quite why they feed on such an unnaturally behaving object is beyond me. Would *you* eat a fried fish seen floating gently along the main street at some distance above the ground?

I haven't said much about hooks, because no notable advances have been made by the tackle trade, but I will say something about unhooking pike. I now consider this 'problem' totally solved, and the business or carrying a Middle Ages surgeon's tool kit is quite unnecessary. All you need is a stout canvas glove and a pair of long artery forceps. The fish is laid on its back, you sit *gently* astride its tummy, take the lower jaw in the gloved hand, pull gently, and as the jaws open insert the forceps to remove the hooks. It's as simple as that. Dennis Pye was, I believe, responsible for the germ of the idea but used a rag instead of the glove: Rian Tingay quickly came up with the improved and in my view unbeatable velvet glove technique.

There has been considerable debate in the angling press recently about the use of barbless hooks and super instant strike rigs for pike, some even claiming a 75% success rate for strikes on instant strike rigs, a figure I consider woefully bad. If anglers would use *small* trebles as advocated in Chapter 5 they would find both hook penetration and hook removal quite easy. I simply cannot go along with the idea of barbless hooks: my 31½-pounder most certainly would have got off the hooks at the time it tail-walked, if not before that. Instant hook rigs I am in favour of in principle; it's just that I consider mine as instant as you can reasonably get. However, I'm happy to be converted on this question.

Some people's hooking problems arise when they pick up a tatty rod to do the job with, and the same applies to casting. The rod should be long enough when bait fishing to pick up all the slack line clear of any rubbish, and allow a good, firm sweeping curve to be set in the rod at the same time of striking. The same applies to casting except that when casting small baits (say sprats) long distances it is better to use one of the stiffer fast-taper rods and a 2 oz Arlesey bomb. In fact a 10 feet stepped up carp rod by Olivers of Knebworth, plus an 11 feet SU fast-taper outfit are two bait fishing rods that could cover most of your piking including doubling up for heavy plug and spinner work. Both will throw their appropriate baits (sprat and 4 oz of mackerel) a good 70 yards and that can be important on today's heavily fished waters.

Another effect that heavy fishing may be having on our waters is to force the pike to night feed more often. Of course, not much night fishing has been done in the past, and Ray and I only had the gleam of an idea five years ago, so it may be that pike have always fed during the night. However, I do know one water where night-feeding pike exist now and didn't before, and other waters are certainly producing numbers of good fish in the hours of winter darkness. During the last few winters I've had two 20-pounders after dark, although only in the first hour of darkness. Others have had considerable success around midnight. Even with the possible switch to night feeding, the feeding patterns idea we originally came up with has been borne out all over the country. It is the one totally indisputable fact according to our correspondents, although a majority have fallen head over heels with the hotspot theory, which to me seems sounder today than it did then; even with more intensive piking which tends to spread fish around a bit.

The intensive piking of the last five years is not, of course, entirely a result of the brilliant discourse on pike by the present authors! It is at least partly a result of five extremely mild winters. But some of the activities I have witnessed during this period have made me fear for the future of piking in this country. There is no doubt that the increased enthusiasm of many anglers for the pike, now second only to the roach in popularity according to one survey, has resulted in a rise of resentment from the anti-pike brigade who have always been fairly dormant. Now they are trying to get piking banned (pike banned!) and various legitimate techniques banned. Many of these people are the worst type of match angler who would probably like to see all fishing banned except that between 10 a.m. and 3 p.m. in straight lines on Sundays. But pike anglers are going to have to fight tooth and nail to keep their sport safe both from such people and from misguided pike killers that exist on numerous small club committees.

Another result of the intensive pressure on quality pike fisheries has been to move the quality pike angler to new and distant waters. The Irish, Scottish and Welsh waters are being explored; many of our 'standard' techniques are proving highly successful in Eire, as Ray explains in his new addition to this book (Chapter 15), and great fish are being caught. I had my first Scottish 20-pounder earlier this year, but before long someone will get one of the real giants, a forty pound-plus fish, and we shall enter yet another era of pike angling history. As they say, it's an ill wind . . .

CHAPTER 10

WEATHER CONDITIONS

Ray Webb

When one turns to the correlation between weather and sporting prospects, it is very much a case of studying an intricate, involved subject with so many exceptions to whatever set of rules one might finally arrive at, that there is a definite tendency on the part of many anglers to throw in the towel, giving the whole thing up in disgust. Beyond all doubt, complications do so often set in to an exasperating degree, but in spite of the difficulties encountered a serious attempt to study the subject is well worth making. There are conclusions to be arrived at which can, in spite of frequent exceptions, improve one's prospects of success enormously. For many years I kept a day by day diary of weather conditions, which when read in conjunction with results obtained on the bankside showed several very definite conclusions, though a certain type of weather which could so often see tremendous catches on one water might well cancel out all hope at another venue a few short miles away. Having compared experiences both verbally and by correspondence with other pike enthusiasts, further confusion is thrown on the matter when one realizes that not only does the water to be fished affect the issue, but also the technique employed as well. On a day when a 5 oz livebait worked along the reedy fringes could confidently be expected to show a good return, a 6 in jointed plug would usually fail altogether and vice-versa. As experience grows, with graphs and statistics mounting up in volume, valuable patterns do in fact emerge.

One of the major factors involved in the feeding behaviour of pike or any other fish too for that matter, is the question of temperature. An accurate thermometer is an extremely worthwhile purchase for any angler's basket. As I flick through the pages of my diaries of seasons past, at the top of every page are two figures, one being the temperature of the water, the other that of the air. It is only by having both readings available that one can predict which way the water temperature is likely to be moving, up or down, this being of course a very pertinent point; just about as important in fact as the reading itself. My experience of summer piking being limited to one short year, I'm unable as yet to form any definite opinions for the warmer months but having been hard at it through the winter, October to March inclusive for fifteen seasons, the facts of the position at this time of year are much more obvious to my way of thinking. Starting off on Hornsea in October the water can be expected to read way up over the 50°F mark and when the water was fishing well consistent results were the order of the day. Blanks were few and far between, with usually one or two good fish to show, and up to half a dozen or so on occasions. Double-figure pike were regularly taken with always the chance of a 20-pounder thrown in. With the water so extremely warm in the weeks of October however, it was largely a waste of time fishing on through the middle of the day, being very much a case of rowing as fast as one could to the chosen swim, an 8 a.m. kick-off being in force, baits out as quickly as possible in the hope of picking up a pike before the sun developed full power. There was then a long period of complete inactivity till feeding commenced once more just as dusk approached. It really was astonishing how often the only run of the morning came at or around 10 a.m. I well remember the scepticism on Tag Barnes' face as I instructed him to set his alarm for that hour. He didn't exactly tell me in so many words to pull the other leg but that was certainly the message implied. Yet I was to have the last laugh on this and many other occasions, for sure enough within seconds of the striking of the hour, the line started to peel steadily off the spool of one of the rods in use. From that point on I noticed Tag tended to pay considerably more attention to any theory I might be inclined to put forward regardless of how unlikely it might at first appear.

As the season progressed into November however, rapidly falling temperatures taking the thermometer down to around 40°F brought about a considerable alteration in the feeding pattern. 10 a.m. as a witching hour became a thing of the past. It was usually 11 or even 12 o'clock before sport would commence but, once having started, a run was very much on the cards at any time of the afternoon right through until dusk saw us heading away from the water. By the beginning of December, winter weather in deadly earnest was usually upon us and the going on Hornsea became rough, very rough indeed, which was only to be expected on a shallow, exposed lake with a maximum depth of around eight feet and most of it three feet or so or less than that. Many times, after several hours sitting quietly in a punt way out on the Mere around late January or early February, with a searching east wind coming off the North Sea seemingly all the way from the Steppes of Russia, I've been convinced that this must surely be the coldest spot in the British Isles. I could well understand the pike having little or no interest in food. There is always some sort of chance of picking up the odd fish and on Hornsea this could mean a big one but it was long odds against the angler in these conditions. It had, however, only to see a sudden rise in temperature taking the water up from 35°F to 40°F or thereabouts to present a very different picture. Sport could then become very hectic and I don't mean the odd fish either; in late February of 1963 for instance Johny Neville and I arrived to find the water remarkably warm at 42°F, fished really hard for two full days, and boated twenty-two pike between us including a 20-pounder to John, the first I'd seen, up to then, that reached the magical weight. About the same time, however, I was doing quite a lot of fishing on the Great Ouse near Littleport and to bear out the point about a given set of weather conditions affecting two different waters in two different ways I found that the very best time of all to employ the ledgered herring, precisely the same technique as was used on Hornsea, was in settled spells of anti-cyclonic weather when clear blue skies gave a tremendous drop in overnight temperatures leaving the banks coated hard with frost the following morning. Travelling down from Sheffield once early in the morning, just such conditions obtained. It was a real nightmare of a journey with the old van skidding about all over the road, yet four good pike found their way to the net going 8 lb, 12 lb, 15 lb and 15¼ lb; my personal best bag for one day up to that time. Operating in similar conditions on the same water with some regularity, it was borne out time and time again, bitter cold weather would see the best results coming to ledgered herring. Perhaps the most striking example of all came on Thursday, January 20th, 1966, a day when the temperature sank so low that the sea itself froze over at Herne Bay in Kent, yet I still managed, after finding one short stretch of water that remained ice free, on account of a push of water coming in at this point, to steer an extremely lively 22¼-pounder all the way to the net.

After temperature, if there is one other condition of weather that I could choose for a day's piking it would be fog, the thicker the better. I've a lot of faith in a real pea-souper and not just for pike either. My best returns with chub on the Trent for example were taken when I could hardly see the end of the rod. On Hornsea once again, the scene of so many of my most memorable days with the pike, it was so thick with fog one day that the 20 minutes row across the lake did on this occasion take over 45 minutes. I'd travelled very nearly completely round in a circle at one stage arriving almost back where I started. In spite of the late start to the actual fishing as a consequence, sport was really brisk; five fish for 76 lbs being a good return on any water. Obviously the pike had no trouble locating the bait even if I couldn't see where I was going.

Down on the Norfolk Broads sport could be extremely good when the visibility was down to a mere ten yards or so. One occasion when Dennis Pye was out doing a feature for *Angling Times* for instance saw five big pike taken in quick time on a day when fog was lying heavy on the water. Livebaiting on the Ouse too in such conditions can really pay dividends yet discussing foggy weather with Fred Wagstaffe, a man with vast experience and knowledge of pike fishing, I was surprised to hear that he's got to the stage where he hardly considers it worth while fixing up the tackle in these sort of conditions. It's significant perhaps that Fred is an ardent artificial man, having no regard at all for deadbaiting and not a deal more for the time-honoured use of livebait. It could well be that his rapidly moving spoons and plugs are difficult for the pike to detect when foggy weather is about, though with his technique being at its very best in the warmer summer months, very little fishing time should be lost I'd imagine.

Often accompanying a thick foggy condition, ice on the water is regarded with mixed feelings as a rule. Some swear by it; some swear at it and many anglers leave their rods in the holdall when ice has formed to any noticeable degree. In my experience once again so much depends on what type of water one intends to fish and also how much ice there is about. With just a marginal freeze-up the Great Ouse has provided me with some really top class sport but this of course is running water and artificially warmed running water at that. Many still waters, Hornsea included, seem to go very quiet indeed in these circumstances, only the odd suicidal pike being at all likely, if that. Variable though the effects of ice along the fringes may be, a completely frozen-up water is, in my considerable experience just about as bad a prospect as one could come across. Many times I've heard tell of tremendous catches of fish made fishing in true Eskimo style, through a hole in the ice, but though I've often given it a trial the next success to come my way in this fashion will be the first. In the winter of '62–63 I spent all one day working with chisels, blowlamps, hacksaws and pickaxes on a pond in East Yorkshire, the results of my labours being four small holes of about 2½ feet square. All our subsequent fishing was in vain, not a sign of life could we raise. Perhaps this is hardly a fair example, for that particular winter was not just normally cold but was in fact the severest recently recorded, week after week temperatures remaining at sub-zero levels until just about all forms of life, human life included, went into a state of complete hibernation. If no success with rod and line came my way I did at least achieve some worthwhile results for when the big thaw finally did set in this was the only water in the whole of the area that didn't suffer a heavy fish mortality. My work with the pickaxe got oxygen down to them apparently just when they needed it most. One well-known writer did in fact commit himself in print to saying that when a water is completely iced over a small hole will bring fish round it, large numbers drawn by the high oxygen content of the cleared spot. As a theory it sounds reasonable enough but in practice, my practice that is, it's not as good as it sounds, nothing like as good. Perhaps it's me doing it all wrong but all the fishing I've done points to the marginal strip of ice as being enough, once a water is completely covered I'm inclined to go searching around for one that isn't.

Really strong powerful winds are also inclined to put many anglers off. Beyond all doubt difficulties do arise when a force 'niner' is howling along, but as a man who's made a habit of sticking it out regardless, there is no doubt in my mind that it is only the fishermen who are put off, not the fish. So often have first class results with pike come my way in times of high winds that I now have the utmost confidence if on tackling up, the rod keeps getting blown off the idleback. In Ireland last summer I found the general concensus of opinion in favour of a 'fairly wild sort of a day'. It was certainly that when my 29-pounder came aboard. I was in fact very loath to stand up in the boat at all so difficult was the task of keeping one's balance. On Lough Nafooey too there were white caps to the waves in plenty; we only went there at all because it had been consistently too rough to fish Lough Mask for ten days. In spite of the boat bobbing up and down fit to beat the band Fred Wagstaffe hit up two fine twenty pound plus fish in two days, a really outstanding performance. These were instances of pike feeding well in prolonged spells of rough weather but I've taken particular notice of the fact that a slight breeze, just enough to cause a mere ripple on the surface, coming after a spell of flat calm will regularly set the fish feeding. It was first brought to my notice on Hornsea in October 1965. Several times after a hot, calm afternoon with nothing doing at all, the glassy mirror-like surface would break up before a rising breeze around 4.30 p.m. or thereabouts and straight away both rods would develop a run at the same time. It happened far too often for it to be mere coincidence. Exactly the same thing has happened to me on many other waters as well and not only in the afternoon either. Less than a week ago in fact out at dawn on a Fenland drain the early morning calm was broken as a wind sprang up around 10 a.m. Immediately the waves started to build up, down went the float and out came a 21 lb pike. It certainly pays dividends to be really on the alert in these circumstances. Not only can this condition of rising wind after calm bring the pike on feed, it can also sort them out size-wise too. The first time I had personal experience of this was on Hornsea once again on November 7th, 1964. Two hours of intensive fishing in the calm of early morning left Johnny Neville and myself with nothing to show, but just coming up to 11 a.m. a really powerful wind, no mere breeze this time, had John and I wondering whether we might be well advised to up anchor and head for shelter. The decision as usual was to stay put, however, and just how wise a verdict this was, was to become obvious in a matter of ten minutes or so as I hauled out a fine pike of 20¼ lb my first 20-pounder ever in fact. This was followed immediately by another big one that went 21½ lb. All afternoon the gale raged unabated, the fish fed steadily on and we finished the day with nine pike for 132 lb, every one of them over 10 lb. I'm firmly convinced that the rough weather stirred the bigger pike up into such a spell of intensive feeding that every self-respecting jack in the lake found a quiet spot for itself and lay there doggo till the danger was past.

Something similar in the way of an intensive feed spell is often triggered off too by a thunder and lightning storm. This has been common knowledge in tench fishing for years but just the same thing happens with pike as well. Chatting up some of the Irish pike enthusiasts, and such people do exist, they are not all trout and salmon only men, I was told that great sport was regularly experienced during an electric storm. The waters they fish are so big it is hardly wise to stay out on the lake if one is known to be approaching. It often happens however that they are taken completely unawares, in which case a bait might just as well be trolled along behind the boat running fast for shelter as not. Unfortunately (or is it?) a savage take is so often met with that the flashing and banging overhead gets completely ignored: angling in earnest being taken up once again and I've very little doubt that, foolhardy or not, I should do much the same thing myself.

These then are some of the general conclusions I've arrived at after 14 years of all-out effort in search of pike. There is no doubt in my mind that they hold true on the waters I've fished. Other anglers operating on different fisheries may well have found just the opposite to hold good for, as I've said already, the relationship between the weather and fish feeding behaviour is an exceedingly complex one. It is well worth putting in a lot of time and effort to understand for all that. No one could, or in fact would, fish every day but an angler of knowledge and experience can when setting out for a day on the bankside weigh up the conditions prevailing at the time and come up with a decision on where to fish and what method to employ. This will nine times out of ten give him an extremely good chance of obtaining really first class sport.

II

In order to actually record weather conditions it is a help to have some equipment—yet more things to carry. However, all that is needed is a thermometer, a light-meter and a barometer. I shall tackle the business of barometric pressure and piking later in this chapter, and suffice it to say about light-meters that I have never managed to sport one for photographic purposes let alone fishing. Such factors as sun, cloud and wind have to be recorded with a good eye as far as I am concerned. We are left with the problem of a thermometer. Various angler's thermometers are available nowadays, yet they all seem a little expensive to me. I use a little tiny alcohol thermometer that goes by the brand name of 'Autotherm'. The cost at one of the chain stores, Woolworths I think, is not unreasonable, which, considering the rate at which I lose small items of tackle, is just as well for me. First of all I check my buy against a sophisticated laboratory thermometer, then I carefully wrap up any breakable edges in Elastoplast, and finally I drop it into an old foam-lined case. In such a condition it can be thrown thirty yards with no risk of breakage. I lose mine by leaving them in the water after taking the temperature or by treading on them when paddling in the shallows. Like trout fishermen, pike anglers also like to paddle.

I very much doubt whether any pike angler of the future will discover a temperature band in which all pike in all waters are on the feed. The whole point about noting water and air temperature is, as Ray says, to ascertain the pattern for *your* water. The same goes for other weather factors as well, except for barometric pressure, as I shall explain shortly.

There is *one* definite correlation between pike and water temperature, and that concerns fighting ability. On all waters of my experience the pike fight less well when the water temperature drops to around 40°F. This happens long before pike become heavy with spawn, and it is a good water where the pike battle well after November. There are always exceptions, individual fish that would fight if frozen solid, but in general the rule holds. I usually find that anglers who claim that 'their' water holds the hardest-fighting pike in Britain have only fished for them in summer. Some of the colder, faster rivers, and some of the wilder lochs and loughs may be exceptions, in that pike quite used to cold water, and pike that have never heard a human footfall always tend to fight well.

An example taken from the autumn of 1970 will suffice to illustrate the fall off in fighting ability. Between October 1st and the beginning of November I had a considerable number of hard fighting double-figure pike, to all methods, and including a number of 20-pounders. The last two twenties in this spell were taken on successive casts and weighed 20½ and 26 lb respectively. Both fell to half-mackerel ledgered at sixty yards' range, and both gave tremendous battles, the smaller fish giving me the greatest battle I have ever had with any fish. On a typical run the fish would take ten to fifteen yards of line, pause for a split second, and, before I could even think of pumping it back, take another ten or fifteen yards. At one point in the fight I had eighty yards of line off the spool, and was beginning to think about losing my first 30-pounder. ... It took a full fifteen minutes before it charged at full speed into a half-sunken landing net.

Still trembling and aching I unhooked the half-mackerel from its lower jaw, and looked up just in time to see a column of spray about sixty yards away as a hunting pike lashed at the surface over fifteen feet of water. I quickly popped the 20-pounder into a keepnet, and, using the same tackle and half-mackerel, punched the bait out to the feeding fish. About five minutes later, during which time I had recovered somewhat, I saw the line streaming off the spool and the float nowhere in sight. Another hefty strike, this time into a fish almost eighty yards' distant, and another powerful fight lasting about seven or eight minutes and the 26-pounder finally hit the net. Ray had done the 'double' several years ago, and it was really great to tell him about this catch.

Three weeks later the water temperature was down around 40°F and the pike came in like lambs, relatively speaking anyway. The same thing happens every year on most of the waters I fish, but I am not certain whether the 'rule' applies to waters like Lough Ree.

A final comment on really low temperatures is prompted by Ray's remarks about Hornsea Mere and the bitterly easterly winds which so often seem to sweep it. I remember spending two long days there one winter, two days without a run, and with a searing and constant easterly blast. At around 4 p.m. on the second day, just when I got a faint feeling that we might get a run on herring, one of the boat's occupants who was huddled on the bottom boards like the rest of us, started sobbing. We should have realized much earlier, when he went quiet in fact, that he was suffering from exposure. This is the nearest we have ever come to losing someone through exposure to the elements, and it certainly isn't a matter to be taken lightly even in England. Under such extreme weather conditions the right sort of clothes are important: a modicum of common sense is better still.

Pike and light conditions make an interesting study. Ray has already mentioned thick fog, and my experiences are similar to his. Fog in the fens fills one with confidence. It is also true that many waters go well at dawn and dusk when the light is weakest: most pike anglers arrive two hours after dawn and leave one hour before dark. Some of our leading anglers have made the same observations about roach, and, indeed, it may be the feeding activities of this and other food fishes which helps to set the pike feeding. There are certainly risks of circular arguments here, and yet both pike and big roach may come on the feed because they need the cover of semi-darkness.

We had a very impressive case of light affecting the feeding pike on December 26th, 1970. Several of the Cambridgeshire Pike Anglers were fishing a fenland drain under quite bright, even sunny conditions. By 11.30 a.m. we had very little to show for $3\frac{1}{2}$ hours of effort when a snow storm blotted out the rosy scene for about fifteen minutes. During that time we had six runs on ledgered herrings and mackerel resulting in fish of $13\frac{1}{2}$ lb; $18\frac{1}{2}$ lb; $14\frac{1}{4}$ lb; and $10\frac{1}{2}$ lb, plus two dropped baits. One of the runs actually stopped as the sun came out again. We had no more runs for a long period, until the bright sun faded, in fact. Then followed fish of 14 lb; $14\frac{3}{4}$ lb; $9\frac{1}{2}$ lb and $11\frac{1}{4}$ lb. Pike anglers who dismiss this sort of thing as coincidence will miss a lot of pike.

Night fishing for pike is here to stay and can reasonably be considered under the title of light conditions! Whether we will ever be able to predict *when* to night fish, I don't know. After all it takes us all our time to predict when to day fish. Perhaps on some heavily fished waters *any* night fishing may yield results at first.

I'm thinking here of a water such as Landbeach near Cambridge. Nowadays it yields few big pike but plenty of fish from 1–3 lb weight, and it is heavily flogged for these. One day during the 1966 winter I watched ten baits at work in one small deepish bay, the total result for a full day being a few fish up to four pounds. After dark when the rest of the anglers had packed up I stayed on for several hours. I should point out that I was after pike-perch at the time and used scaled down pike gear, including tiny livebaits under 1 in diameter floats, at a depth of about three feet. I had two or three small pike in the first two hours after dark, followed by a fish of 11 lb after three hours' fishing, a veritable monster of the water at this time. On subsequent trips we got our pike-perch and numbers of pike. It became clear that on this water the fish fed as freely after dark as during daylight hours. Conditions on each occasion were overcast, the only blank being on a bright moonlit night. The only other winter night blanks I have had have been under similar conditions, perhaps because there is usually a considerable drop in temperature, particularly if the day has been sunny. This fishing has been done only during the first few hours of darkness, since at that time I was neither mentally nor physically equipped to cope with a full, long winter-night session. I intend to do a lot more however. Summer night-fishing I suspect will turn out to be less spectacularly successful, if only because the pike have plenty of time to feed during the day. Small pike certainly feed well on some summer nights as every tench angler knows too well.

In my very early days of pike fishing I was quite unable to get results under really windy conditions, and to tell you the truth I preferred flat calm water surfaces where my large bung could be seen for miles. I now know that some of the waters I fished *do* fish well in those glassy calms, particularly on early summer's mornings before the sun is up. I also know that my skill at tackle control was unable to face fishing in a strong north-westerly gale. Nowadays I prefer a stiff breeze, particularly if it does not impede tackle control or casting too much, and it is quite surprising how often the wind can be made to work for you. Wind is a great asset if the pike angler wants to drift a suspended deadbait, or make a float-ledgered deadbait drag slowly round in a wide arc.

I used to have a nasty little ruse to get round choppy conditions on some small pike waters: as I say *any* wind was detrimental when I first started. This consisted of tying some cord around a half pound block of margarine, setting it to the depth of the water, putting a stone on the other end and then heaving it out into some unobtrusive spot in the lake where it remained anchored to the bottom. Within a short time the choppy lake surface was reduced to a glossy if somewhat oily calm. I rather think that this technique might be frowned upon today, and would not encourage it as part of your repertoire. I discovered it, incidentally, when mashing up sandwiches into groundbait which was then heaved around the pike bungs.

Smooth conditions are not necessarily detrimental to success as so many pundits seem to think. Indeed, if the light is poor, I am usually quite confident, other things being equal. Suspended deadbaits work well on glassy calm still waters, contrary to the popular idea that foot-high waves are required to give a suspended deadbait 'life'. Even under rough conditions the pike is quite fully aware that a suspended deadbait is stone dead, as evidenced by the fact that they will often prefer suspended deadbaits to suspended livebaits under both rough and calm conditions. Equally often they prefer the livebaits. The rough water has nothing whatever to do with the success of the dead as opposed to the livebait, of that I am certain.

From what has been written above it must be clear to the reader that in the writer's opinions nothing in the way of weather characteristics will form a key as to whether pike will be on the feed over a wide area. The great advantage of weather study in relation to pike is that it helps *you* to work out the pattern for *your* waters. Never believe that definite recognizable patterns do not exist.

Having said that I shall return, with some unease, to the subject of barometric pressure and big pike. First of all there are several problems to think about, and I can provide no answers. One is that pike should not know anything about atmospheric pressure changes. After all water was incompressible when I was a schoolboy, and I understand it still is. And again, most pike traverse considerable depths: they will often come up from the bottom in twenty feet of water and take a livebait fished two feet deep. When they do this the water pressure upon their bodies must change dramatically. Why should they worry about relatively

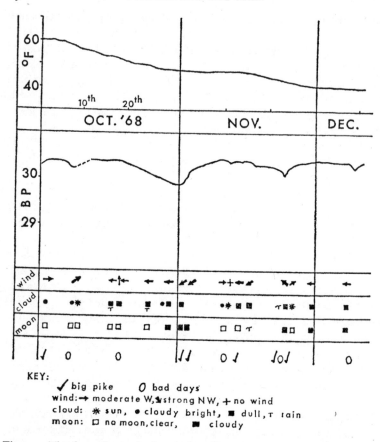

Fig. 22. The bare facts of 2½ months pike trips plotted graphically and pictorially, thus releasing the normal diary for ideas, feelings, conclusions etc.

minute atmospheric pressure changes? I can offer no answers, except to suggest that pike, and other fish, living in the dense medium of water, may be acutely perceptive of what appear to us as tiny changes in conditions.

I will say categorically that there *is* a relationship, probably a direct relationship, between the feeding of big pike and the pressure patterns. This being the case one would expect pressure to have a wide geographical effect on feeding since a trough may embrace the whole of Britain at once, whereas sunshine, wind, cloud cover, fog, frost and all the other variables are essentially local features even within a single pressure system. I think this is actually the case: how often do we read in the angling press of a 'pike week', or a 'bream week' for that matter, when all the pike in the country seem to be on the feed? Editors and newspaper men have assured me that they do not hold back information in order to make a 'pike week', so *something* brought the pike in general on the feed. I would contend that it is *not* temperature, or rain, or cloud cover etc. since these are so variable from area to area. In fact, the pike have responded to widespread, controlling barometric pressure regions.

It seems to me that when there is a sudden, big, sustained pressure rise after, say, two or three weeks when the barometer has been either very low or very variable, then the pike came on the feed with a vengeance. A sustained very low pressure regime, sustained for a week or more, often sends the fenland pike quite 'off' moving baits such as livebaits and spinners, and yet many feed exceptionally well on ledgered herrings and mackerels. I am a practical angler, not a theorist, and it is fortunate that these ideas are based not so much upon watching press reports for several years, but upon the capture by myself and eight friends of over 500 pike in excess of 10 lbs in three years. I *know*, on our waters, that excessive, sustained, low pressures will result in the pike feeding well on ledgered herrings. Big pressure rises tend to make them forget herrings and hunt more actively for livebaits. The Christmas weekend of 1970, for example, was accompanied by a marked, but not sustained low-pressure regime, and several of us on a fen drain had nearly twenty runs on ledgered mackerel resulting in about 15 pike over 10 pounds, and one of 20½ lbs to Mick Griffiths. Less than half this number of runs were obtained on livebaits and these were mostly small fish around 4–8 lb. Had the low pressure been more sustained it would have been unusual to get any runs on livebaits.

Just recently I have heard from Dr. Terence Coulson, the well known angler–physicist, that the National Anguilla Club have instigated, at my suggestion, barometric pressure studies. Already they have noted a marked correlation between pressure and eel feeding spells, without as yet having carried out statistical tests. Terry Coulson also considers that the graphs I have kept for several years are strongly suggestive of a relationship between pressure and pike (and other species). Some anglers with whom I

have discussed these problems have suggested that the relationship might not be *direct*, but might involve a linked system
such as phytoplankton to food fish to pike. Clearly, ideas of this
kind will take some testing but for our purpose the link of B.P.
to pike will do as a working relationship. Fig. 22 gives some actual
examples of results versus pressure graphs. I would just add that
extreme local conditions such as torrential rain, floods, or snow
water may affect the piking more strongly than what I now regard
as the overall controlling factor, namely barometric pressure.
That the picture may be yet more complicated than the way I
have painted it, is suggested by the fact that on some of our local
drains even a rapidly rising barometer may bring the fish on the
feed on one section of the system only!

Standard barometers, normally adorning hallways or doctors'
surgeries, can be studied before going fishing and after returning.
However, I have a small pocket model, like a folding alarm
clock. This I find is a great deal more convenient than going to
the doctor: the wife refuses to have a barometer hanging in the
hall.

CHAPTER 11

LOCATING BIG PIKE

Ray Webb

As good a starting point as any, in the quest to catch big pike is to find out first of all exactly where they are. Many of the best waters are of course nationally famous: the Norfolk Broads, Hornsea Mere, the Hampshire Avon, Loch Lomond up over the border in Scotland. These and other venues too are familiar to all who go fishing at all, but 20 lb pike are not restricted to the well-known waters only. They are in fact fairly widespread in distribution. Once a short-list of likely spots has been compiled, probably the best policy is to select one or two waters that can be fished regularly, twice a week say or more if possible, then really stick at it until results start to come as they certainly should inside a season or two. By constantly haunting a fishery in this fashion the angler gets to know the water in all its moods, low and gin clear in early October, up over the banks and thickly coloured in November, fringed with ice at Christmas; knowledge built up in this way will surely pay dividends to the perceptive angler who sticks to the job in hand. If anything really hot develops elsewhere, something obviously too good to miss, as happened on Horsey two or three years ago, then by all means nip over and have a go but failing that sort of golden opportunity, then stick to the one or two waters selected. It is a mistake to go dashing about here there and everywhere trying a different spot every week. I did my share of that sort of thing at one stage but the returns just didn't justify the effort involved.

Once a water has been selected for intensive fishing the next move obviously is to consult the regulars. Men with years of experience of the fishery and an impressive list of big fish captures are the ones to seek out. They don't have to pass on information of course and may often, in fact, deliberately attempt to lead the enquirer up the garden path, but nevertheless it's always a good

133

move to listen to what they have to say, use a spot of judgement as to what makes sense and what doesn't in the light of one's own experience elsewhere, and work from there. Water bailiffs and club officials are also well worth consulting. In many cases one finds that they actually fish very rarely themselves, having more or less retired from practical angling many years previously, but they do keep in touch with current developments on the fishery and this being so can frequently come up with extremely worthwhile information. A trip along to the nearest pub can also turn out to be quite an investment since in addition to the usual benefits derived, it is more than likely that a glass-case specimen or two will adorn the walls. Publicans as a rule are well aware of the trade-pulling power of such objects, and conversation can so easily be turned in this direction.

On occasions however, one comes across a water that is rarely fished, generally considered to have been fished out years ago maybe, and virtually nothing of value can be found out from other anglers about the current prospects. When one travels to remote areas, or to trout and salmon fishing districts where pike fishing is rarely practised, the same will apply. Such has happened to me from time to time and in these circumstances undoubtedly the best bet is to launch a boat, have a quick scout round, find out the depths, position of weed beds, inflow and outflow streams and so on, but first and foremost work by depth. For sheer breath-taking speed and efficiency a modern echo sounder which gives not only a visual indication on a meter but also plots a graph as well is in a class of its own. Failing that, the time-honoured plumb-line will do the job and if not so quickly or effectively, it will at least give something to work on. My own introduction to the echo sounder came in the company of Bob Reynolds and Fred Wagstaffe, two very knowledgeable and highly successful pike men, on a water of some two miles or so in length by perhaps three-quarters of a mile wide, way out in the back of beyond where we literally had no hope of outside help. It was very much a case of reading the water's potential for ourselves. Quickly launching their thirteen-feet boat, Black Pig, equipped with two sounders, we did an initial run straight down the middle, another round the shoreline, plus one or two criss-crosses, and in a matter of a mere hour or two there was a map of the depth contours that would have taken a full day's work or more to

compile by the old traditional method. Three-quarters or more of
the lake proved to be eighty feet or more in depth, being written
off straightaway, but one small corner, sheltered from the prevailing wind by an island, turned out to have a moderate amount
of weed growing in six feet or so of water with the odd drop off
down to sixteen or eighteen feet. Much more to our liking, a start
was made here. Just how wise a decision this was became apparent inside two or three days for in that short space of time, on a
new and unknown fishery, Fred took a fine brace of pike that went
$22\frac{1}{2}$ and $23\frac{1}{4}$ lb, as dramatic an instance of the value of working
by depth as one could ever hope to come across. As a broad
generalization water of three to twenty feet or so is the most
productive, the pike moving from the shallower end of this
range towards the deeper as the water temperature drops down
to its winter level. One article did appear once in the angling
press about pike from eighty feet down, a number of really good
catches being made on small spinners fishing at this depth, but
this is the only instance I ever heard of when pike were taken so
far down. It can perhaps be classified as the exception that
proves the rule. Places where the bottom slopes away from
shallow to deeper water, as in the case quoted where Fred succeeded so well, are always worth particular attention and a good
weed bed or two will also show a good return providing, as it
does, cover for the pike to lie in ambush. On the Norfolk Broads,
a livebait worked close in along the reedy fringes has for many
years yielded tremendous results to Dennis Pye, and the margins
of pondweed too in my own experience have given up some very
good catches.

Inflow streams and outflows are also well worth an extended
trial. The deeper I go into this pike fishing game the more I
become convinced that the old theory of still or slack water for
Esox is only half-way correct at the most. No doubt about it,
many of our lakes and reservoirs produce extremely big pike in
numbers but there is, in my experience at any rate, quite a case
to be built up for seeking out the fastest, most turbulent water
around before fixing up tackle in earnest. One slow and deep
stretch of water that I fished regularly, had at one time a considerable reputation for big pike but for all the good fish that I
caught or saw anyone else take there it began to look like another
fisherman's tale. Chatting up a local one day, I was advised to

move some three-quarters of a mile or so upstream to the pump-house, where excess water was lifted off the low-lying land and pushed into the river at high speed (Fig. 23). Undoubtedly, the hottest spot on the river for pike I was told. 'They like the push of water on their backs you know'. It was the first time I'd ever heard anyone put forward the idea of pike as a lover of fast water but I decided to give it a try, the results obtained so far

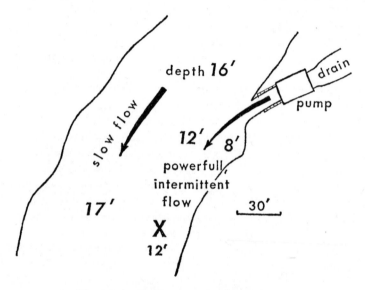

Fig. 23. A pike hotspot on a Fenland river.

putting me in the position of really having nothing to lose. From the very first attempt it was obvious that the local man knew what he was talking about. Double-figure pike began to come to the net with ever-increasing frequency, there really was a tremendous concentration of pike in the twenty or thirty yards' stretch below the outflow. Eventually a 23½-pounder was taken here, not by myself unfortunately, but by a guest that we introduced to the swim. He was fishing a livebait close into the edge, and the fish was a really solid, heavily-built specimen. From this day on I kept a look-out for similar spots and eventually started to fish a stretch where the flow, in time of high water levels, really surged along, as unlikely a stretch for big pike as could be imagined in view of the old slack water for *Esox* theory. Once again the pike were found to be concentrated right in the strongest push of water around, not just 3 lb or 4 lb jack but fish of all sizes: small, medium and big were crowded together into one enormous pack. It could be argued that the pike were there because of the shoals of roach, perch and bream that were always present at these spots, and there may well be something in that, but I always felt that the old local had hit the nail on the head; they really did like to feel the flow of water on their backs. Whatever the facts of the situation, whenever I fish a still or slow-moving water for pike these days, if there is a short stretch anywhere with a really fierce push of current, then failing any other information to work on, that is the spot where I make a start. It is not just in the warmer weather either; these streamy swims hold pike in numbers right through the depths of winter.

There is no doubt in my mind that pike and other species too come to that, are none too keen on excessive bankside disturbances or having boats in numbers churning the water up above their heads day after day, week after week. If this sort of thing takes place regularly on a fishery the pike will often seek out a quiet secluded spot and congregate there, affording the angler who is quick to realize what has happened with a really outstanding prospect.

By far the great majority of the pike caught by Barrie and myself on Hornsea were taken as a result of hammering away at one spot on the Mere for circumstances had congregated 90 per cent and more of the lake's pike into this particular stretch. For donkey's years the Mere had been very lightly fished indeed and surface disturbances negligible, the pike being caught at all points round the lake by the few anglers who fished for them. At one period the deep trough by the island, seven feet that is, for it is a shallow water of four to five feet generally, produced the big ones regularly, and about Christmas time or just after the roach shoals moved to the boathouse gathering under the boats and jetties till the water was black with them. They could, and were, scooped out in landing nets to be used for livebait for the pike that hovered around just off the end of the jetties; the hottest spot of all at that time for the closing weeks of the season. The situation changed however, when, from being a lightly fished members only water, boats became available for all and the yachting enjoyed such a tremendous boom, regular races being held that covered practically all the fishable area of the Mere. Week in and week out, season after season, the water was churned up by the intensive boat traffic till the pike decided that they had had enough and moved away up the lake to the sanctuary, a short stretch reserved for wild life.

Catches had been far from impressive for several seasons till a decision was made to row the measured mile across the lake to the sanctuary boundary, a gamble that paid off one of the richest piking dividends it has ever been my good fortune to experience. From the very word go it was action all the way, a 10½-pounder being taken virtually straightaway. The Mere started a glorious spell of sport that was to continue for three whole seasons before the returns registered a rapid decline. Beyond all shadow of doubt those pike had stood all they were prepared to stand in the way of surface disturbance, retreating to the sanctuary where they had only the birds and no boats to contend with. Much the same thing happens on rivers and drains from time to time though in these cases it is the commotion caused by hordes of anglers tramping along the banks that the fish object to. At the point where road bridges span these waters and the cars and coaches deposit their passengers, the regularly repeated disturbance often tends to drive the pike into the quieter swims between the bridges, where the angler who is prepared to hump his tackle a mile or more along the bank can enjoy first-class sport: far superior to that likely to be obtained by the man who drops in at the first spot he comes to. Bridges over water are well worth seeking out provided they are not subjected to this frequent excessive bankside activity, for the shoal of small fry that usually takes up residence immediately downstream of the arches can be relied to attract a good pike or two. It is only the more popular dropping-off spots that are best avoided.

In addition to locating the pike horizontally as one might say, their position in the vertical plane has also to be accurately assessed if the water's full sporting potential is to be realized. The pike vary the depth at which they will feed from water to water and also from month to month. Fred Wagstaffe assures me that a small lure fished right up in the surface layer during the summer months will, providing there is little or no wind about to put a chop on the water, regularly produce really outstanding results and he is a man with a record of many successes in such conditions.

Though I've no personal experience of surface lures for pike, subsurface fishing is something I've tried with success when using livebait. In my early seasons I'd habitually fished livebait just off the bottom in the manner usually recommended but a day on a water near Cambridge in October 1965 convinced me that there were exceptions to this generally correct rule. With dusk rapidly drawing near and not a pike to show, Barrie and I got to chatting up two local anglers who were already leaving for home though their rods were still fixed up ready for use. From the bounce to their gait as they approached I could see the day had gone well with them and sure enough they had taken fish of 16 and 17 lb around midday, a 19-pounder the previous trip and one over 20 just as the season opened. A glance at their tackle showed there was no finesse involved, short powerful solid glass rods, large floats taking two or three outsize leads and line that looked somewhere around the 30 lb b.s. mark. Pointing out a partly severed spot which had presumably been caught between a pike's teeth I was told not to worry, the remaining bit was probably about 15 lb b.s. and I could well believe it. Certainly they'd no advantage over us in the way of superior tackle, or livebaits either for that matter, but whereas we'd been fishing eleven feet deep in twelve feet of water, their floats were set so the baits were working at a maximum depth of five feet, if that. Commenting that this was against all the normally recommended practice they assured us that the pike would come up to seven feet to take these subsurface baits if indeed they weren't already stationed at that depth anyway which seemed more than likely. Next weekend we were back on the water, floats set at four to five feet and before I'd assembled my tackle Barrie was into a fish which took with a surge that almost lifted it clear of the water, a well-conditioned pike of $18\frac{1}{4}$ lb; followed by another of $16\frac{3}{4}$ lb shortly afterwards; as convincing an initial trial of subsurface fishing as one could wish for, the matter being clinched beyond all shadow of doubt the following day when I took a fine brace of $15\frac{1}{4}$ and $20\frac{1}{4}$ lb in weight. In addition Barrie had eight more to $11\frac{1}{2}$ lb over the two-day period while I had to be content with just one, a tubby little 7-pounder. All 13 pike were taken at four to five feet depth, baits presented ten or eleven feet down were completely ignored. Even more surprising, to me at any rate, was the run that produced, of all things, an eel of 2 lb exactly; that one must surely have come up from the bottom to take the bait since eels do not cruise around at subsurface levels, or do they? Calm conditions are not necessary for this technique to be effective. Barrie's initial successes were achieved with a fair gale blowing. What we did find, however, was that once the water temperature had dropped down, about mid-November, we had to go down to eight feet or more for our pike. It was only during the five or six weeks from October 1st that subsurface fishing really paid dividends. It is a tremendous advantage if the line is well greased to float for this technique otherwise the bait, constantly rising to the surface and falling back down again, tends to produce a series of tangles.

This question of pike location can, and often does, become very obscure and involved, much hard work questing around being necessary before an assessment as to their whereabouts can be made. In spite of all the difficulties encountered however, a really serious attempt to form some sort of opinion is well worth making, a few yards out in the positioning of the bait will often mean the difference between failure and success.

II

I heartily endorse the fundamental principles of big pike location outlined in the first part of the chapter, and would add the Rivers Wye and Hull, and certain Irish rivers, to the list of those producing big pike in fast water. Even on slower streams the really big fellows are often found in the fast water of weirpools, admittedly with slacks often at hand. When Christine, Ray and I did a reconnaissance trip up the River Hull by boat, on a sunny wintry day, we found more fish in the 20-pound bracket in the faster water than we did in the deeper slower reaches, even allowing for the better visibility in the former. In the slower water we noted plenty of roach, and the odd bream, and a few moderate-sized pike. As we neared the northern end of the tidal reaches big pike were more and more in evidence. This was a case of direct observation: the boat would glide slowly over the fish which often hardly moved even when the depth was as little as five feet. It is often impossible to see big pike from the shore or banks, their camouflage is so good. When directly above them at close range camouflage seems less effective at times. I reckon we saw fifteen twenty-pound plus fish that day, with a similar number of double-figure fish, but Ray thought at the time I had probably over-estimated their weights somewhat, possibly as a result of being *too* close to them. Anyway there were tens of big pike of normal colouring, some dark ones starkly outlined against a gravelly bottom, and one striking, almost white pike of some twenty pounds. This last fish lay not on a chalky gravel bottom where it might have been nearly invisible, but on a dark silt and weed bottom, adjacent to some common reed beds, where it stood out like some great aquatic ghost. Probably, at that size, it was not concerned about competition, and thought it could overhaul any foolish roach that came near. Big pike are probably most efficient predators, expending little effort in the kill, for although they are often slightly inaccurate at the point of strike, their sheer speed and power must enable them to overhaul most food fish with some ease.

I mentioned the odd white pike above, and by way of an aside here I would mention some other oddities that turn up from time to time. Firstly pike with the lower jaw upturned at the tip like the kype of a salmon. We have had three of these from the River Great Ouse, one fish of around 3 lb having the three inches of jaw at the tip almost at right angles to the normal rake of the jawline. Playing this fish to the bank was an odd experience for it had a strange resistance in the water. Two-tone pike, exactly similar and just as spectacular as the Irish two-tone bream, have also turned up in the Great Ouse, and both these types of oddity (two-tone and kyped pike) were caught in swims yielding very big pike. This is probably no guide of any kind, but a fact nevertheless. Then there are the rarer 'tubular' pike, in which the front half of the fish, instead of having an oval cross section (in a vertical sense) is perfectly round like a drain-pipe, while the rear half is quite normal. The best one we saw weighed 18 lb and was caught in the Yorkshire Derwent by a friend of Ray.

The white pike that I mention was lying near a large reed bed, and there is no doubt that reed beds have an attraction for big pike. But not just any old common reed bed, not in my experience anyway. For example, most extensive beds of the common reed

(*Phragmites communis*) are rooted in relatively shallow water, say less than eighteen inches, and where they are so rooted the stems are very close together and the debris between the stems considerable. Less commonly they are rooted in up to four feet of water (compare Figs. 24a and 24b) and the stems are widely spaced: almost wide enough to spin through easily. Other things being equal these are the places to look for big pike. Some of the hotspots on Lough Ree are fringed with just such reed beds,

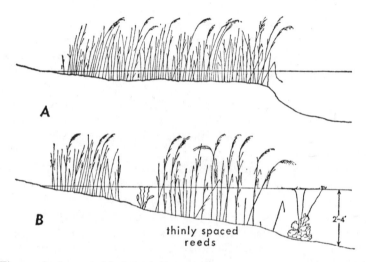

Fig. 24. A; dense reed beds in shallow water: not usually a good pike margin. B; margin with sparse reeds in which pike can get good cover.

unlike many of the margins of the Lough. *The* hotspot of Hornsea Mere was exactly adjacent to one of these reed beds, and, indeed, not only did many big ones run into the reeds upon taking the bait but quite a lot were caught *in* the reeds. On the Norfolk Broads a very similar situation obtains, and some of the experienced livebait anglers on Hickling allow their baits to work deeply into the reeds risking everything in an attempt to get the big ones out. Strong winds are supposed to drive pike from the reed beds into the open water, at least on the Broads, but I was never too happy about this on the Irish waters having seen good pike deep in the reeds with the reed stems really lashing around.

There are a few other tips on pike location which may not,

however, locate only big pike. These are non-selective then, and the best one of all is to trace the fry and small-fish shoals. The East Yorkshire, Lincolnshire and Fenland drain systems are ideal for this kind of approach, for being shallow the shoals can usually be spotted priming quite commonly. Mile after mile might be covered until a really big shoal is located, but it is the big shoal to search for, not the little ones of a few hundred roach or so. When a big shoal *is* located, particularly if it remains in one short stretch for a week or two, then it will have pike in attendance; and if the techniques of the first half of this chapter have been followed, the chances are that you will have found at least *some* big pike. Such fry and small-fish shoals are often given away by the presence of flocks of gulls, or the persistent diving of grebes. Just as in sea angling in fact. Beware of gulls as indicators, however, for I know several waters where their constant appearance in large flocks merely denotes the proximity of the council refuse tip.

Finally, the old trick of tying large herrings to lengths of cotton and throwing them out into the swim can be tried, I gather with success. The only times I have tried to do this have been when all other methods have failed to show the presence of big pike where I expected them—and the herring and cotton method also failed. Don't forget to tie one end of the cotton to a stick in the bankside's growth and not leave it unconnected as one friend of mine did. The pike obtains a free meal out of this system, and the fact that he has done so is indicated when the angler finds the herring missing from the leading end of the thread.

CHAPTER 12

HOTSPOTS AND THE LAIR THEORY

Barrie Rickards

I begin this chapter with some paradoxes. Of all the aspects of pike fishing dealt with in this book hotspots are probably the most difficult to write about, and yet may be the most important. Whilst many anglers are able to accept that some short stretches or a river or lake are much better than others for roach, few of the pike anglers with whom I have discussed the subject seem aware of the existence of hotspots with respect to pike. The idea dies hard that pike, the 'lone brigands' of many writers, are more or less evenly spread throughout a water. They are not. The food fish are unevenly spread, and so are the pike. Similarly, whereas many roach fishermen accept that certain parts of a particular good swim will be better than others, pike anglers seem blind to the idea when fishing for *their* quarry. The truth is probably that there are far fewer experienced pike anglers than there are experienced roach anglers, and the message has quite simply not been passed on.

During the last decade I have probably read hundreds of articles about pike fishing, and have certainly spent hours pouring through the angling newspapers and magazines. After all this time and effort I can remember but four articles mentioning hotspots. The first was several years ago in the now extinct magazine *Fishing*, I think by John Neville of Eckington near Sheffield, which described a particular tiny hotspot on a large Yorkshire still water. More recently Peter Stone, 'The Oxford Act', writing in the *Angler's Mail* (January 1971) gave the locations of known hotspots in Blenheim Palace lake, and Peter Wheat (*Angling*, February 1969) described hotspots on the Hampshire Avon. None of these attempted to account for the hotspots, which pleases me rather because I myself am usually quite unable to offer rational explanations for them. More important to me was

Photo : Ray Gregory

PLATE II

Barrie Rickards nets double figure pike. Rod is Sportex 10′ glass carp
rod. Note sliding float and bead.

PLATE 12
Moment of truth as another big one is weighed: $22\frac{1}{4}$ lb.

a very short article in an issue of *Angler's Mail* during 1970 by Bill Keal; Keal was clearly thinking of hotspots as a widespread phenomenon, something not considered by the few previous authors, and I found in his remarks, though brief, a flicker of some of my own ideas. Although they may be poorly understood and recognized I think the *fact* of hotspots is inescapable.

Well what are hotspots? It might be better to begin by saying what they are not. They are not, as a rule, those points in a river where the feeder ditch runs in, or the bush overhangs, or where the island provides an eddy. Pike are often found in such places, sometimes several fish may be in residence at once, and whilst the odd fish may make a permanent lair at the place I get the impression that it is more usual for pike to visit such swims for short periods. I remember a swim like this on the Market Weighton Canal near Hull: although many fish were caught by us we never took the same fish twice as far as we knew. This particular place has shoals of fry, as feeder stream mouths often do, and I think that actively hunting pike, individuals, move in on the shoals.

No, hotspots are places where vast numbers of big pike shoal up together when they are not in the grip of a frenzied hunting spree. The urge to spectacular hunting comes to such shoals occasionally, and when it does they spread out far and wide, and it seems that all the river is alive with striking pike. For much longer periods they shoal up tight—just how tight I shall explain —and feed regularly for a very short period on most days, and to do this they do not move far but feed on anything that is unfortunate to be in the area. Many writers seem to be of the opinion that pike only shoal up together towards the end of the season, just prior to spawning. They certainly *do* shoal for spawning, but even more tightly packed groups are the rule in my experience during the summer, autumn and throughout the depths of winter. The angler who has located a hotspot, has recognized the feeding pattern, and who fishes regularly and carefully will consistently take big fish and big catches. Clearly, some examples of hotspots would not come amiss at this point.

Ray knows more about Hornsea Mere in East Yorkshire and Horsey Mere in Norfolk, and will probably expound on this theme, but the former water had a hotspot that lasted about three years (under a tremendous barrage of baits) and which had the dimensions of some thirty yards by twenty in an area adjacent

to some common reed beds rooted in about three feet of water.
The swim was fished by an increasing number of boats, innumerable rods, and the fish eventually spread out under the sheer
hammering they were getting. Finally they hightailed it into the
bird sanctuary. But before the overfishing began huge catches
were made in that very small area including a number of 20 lb
plus fish to Ray, whilst numbers of other boats fishing elsewhere
caught almost nothing, bar the odd jack around 3 lb. This is the
test: a hotspot is identified as much by the lack of fish caught in
the surrounding area, as by the tremendous catches caught in the
actual swim.

A few years ago the members of the Cambridgeshire Pike
Anglers, nine of them, identified a hotspot some twenty to thirty
yards long on a fenland drain. By really squeezing things three
or four anglers could fish the hotspot and the rest fished along
either side of them upstream and down. Usually only two were
in the hotspot, in fact, so that when we consider total catches for
one season, listing them as 'hotspot' versus 'the rest', it was 'the
rest' that actually received most attention—the greater number of
rod-days if you prefer to put it that way. Of eighteen twenty-
pound plus fish we took that year from the drain, fourteen came
from the hotspot. Of the double-figure fish only 15 per cent were
caught *outside* the swim, and we had a lot of double-figure fish.
The sport was tremendous: I cannot understand these people
who claim to get fed up of catching big, hard-fighting pike.
Naturally we took turns in the swim, except when Laurie Manns,
Christine and I were on the water when we crowded in together.
We can fish half a dozen rods on a sixpence and only get them
tangled up when Christine casts a spell on us. It is obvious from
the above that the recognition of a hotspot is more easily achieved
with a number of anglers. Several times on this water the pike
came on the feed 'all over', or in other words they moved out of
the hotspot on the rampage; but mostly, whilst big pike were
taken regularly in the spot itself few were taken even thirty
yards away.

Another way to find hotspots, less efficient than the teamwork
mentioned above but useful for two anglers, is to 'leap frog'
along the bank. Bill Chillingsworth and I were doing this one
winter on a stretch of drain we did not know well when eventually
the leading rod found the fish. We moved into the area, and

beyond it, but the fish were coming from a relatively short stretch of some twenty to thirty yards. It turned out to be a transient hotspot—a short-lived one, but more interesting to us was the fact that one particular place in the swim consistently yielded double-figure fish one after another. This area was about five feet out from the bank in quite shallow water, and if the bait was dropped in an area of some four feet by six then runs could be assured. The best fish weighed 19 lb. Outside this tiny area we had to wait much longer. Both of us have met the same thing in other hotspots. Even so, as long as the angler was in the hotspot area of some twenty to thirty yards of bank he was in with a good chance of consistent sport.

I have already implied that hotspots are very small compared to the size of the water. Hornsea Mere is $1\frac{1}{2}$ miles long, but at the time we fished it there was only one hotspot discovered on the water in spite of heavy fishing. Similarly on Lough Ree, some 19 miles long, the local pike expert assured me that as far as he was concerned there were only about six really tremendous stretches on the lake. Although good fish were picked up everywhere from time to time (hunting pike) he regarded most of the lake as so much barren water. It took him ten to fifteen years to reach his conclusions, and life is too short to argue with him. He put me on to two of his hotspots and I began to take good fish; one of these swims yielded him and his son some huge catches of pike to wagtails and large spoons, the best being a catch of five 20-pounders in one day as well as other good fish. This spot was approximately thirty yards by fifty, and boats away from the vicinity took hardly a fish. Before the other locals found out about it he had taken good catches for almost five years, and even during pike matches he was able to use a powerful outboard to reach the swim well before the others, take a fish or two, and then move away in order to keep it secret.

Most hotspots last from year to year and if fished by careful anglers can yield good sport indefinitely. Hornsea Mere was hammered unlike any water I have ever seen, and it lasted just three years, which is more a tribute to the resilience of its hard-fighting pike than to the common sense of the anglers who fished it. Ray and I were to a large degree responsible for letting the cat out of the bag, a thing we regret to this day. We will never knowingly do it again, for the ruination of a hotspot and often of the whole pike water, is a sad event. Hotspots are the reason for being very very cagy about where you catch your fish: most of the ones I fish now would not last three years.

Well, why do pike choose to shoal up in such a small area on a big water? This is the question to which I have no reasonable answer. I know one or two hotspots that are in the region of some feature like a feeder stream or a sharp bend in the river. These places as it happens harbour shoals of roach and bream. Some of the hotspots on the drains I fish are in the region of huge bream shoals without actually being in the middle of the bream: since it is common to find hotspots on one bank only, it is almost as if they leave a gap for the food fish to swim through when they are rash enough. But equally often there are no signs of roach and bream anywhere near the hotspot, which lends support to the idea that the hunting pike move out of the spot itself when really on the feed. The angler fishing a hotspot regularly will be fishing most of the time when the big pike are not really feeding. It is here, in the pike's lair as it were, that real finesse in piking technique counts. Methods which will easily take hunting pike— trolling, spinning, shallow livebaiting with a large bung and so on—may fail completely when free-line livebait, ledgered livebait and carefully presented stationary deadbaits may score heavily. The shallower the water, the truer the above statement seems to be.

But when the pike decide to feed in earnest the knowledgeable angler will be at the very focus, the starting point, of their feeding spree. Normally they will have a short feeding snack each day and in this case the angler will still be consistently successful (see Chapter 2 on Feeding Patterns).

Now for that tight packing that I mentioned. I have spent some time on a tiny drain which is a mere twenty-one feet wide and several miles long (Fig. 25). One of the hotspots is some sixty yards long—unusually long in fact—but within this stretch is a length of ten yards of bank which has yielded a large number of big double-figure pike to ledgered herrings, livebaits and artificials. The water is about three to four feet deep: you could work out the cubic footage as 4 ft × 30 ft × 21 ft. When it is considered that a big pike is between three and four feet long, you could get ten fish nose to tail in one line, and about the same number in a line side by side across the drain. One hundred big pike in such a small area might be exaggerating a fair bit, but nevertheless the less quantitative expression 'packed like sardines' conjures up the right sort of picture. I well remember Ernest Merrit's description of a vast hotspot shoal that he once found on Hornsea Mere, and it bore a close resemblance to the deductions above: he caught 49 of them.

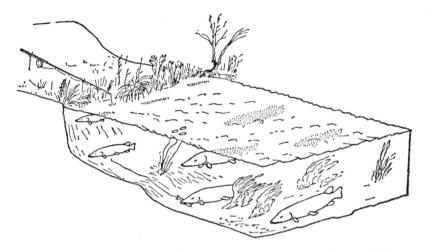

Fig. 25. The author's concept of a hotspot on a small Fenland drain: half the width of the drain is shown, and a depth of about three feet. Such a swim may be twenty yards long, and number *one* for every *two miles* of water.

Obviously the bream shoals cannot often swim the gauntlet past pike concentrations of this nature—it would be suicidal. The pike must go on the hunt. But why then do they stay in one tiny area from season to season? Is it just possible that they ignore bream shoals swimming by until the concentration of them really is more than the pike can stand? As I said at the beginning I have as yet no real reasons for hotspots in most cases, but they exist with a vengeance. Hot swims also survive temporary natural upsets such as floods. On a river when a period of heavy rainfall sets in and water levels rise, poor returns can be expected for a while. Once the dirt and debris clears away a pike or two will usually turn up even if the water remains high. If the flood level persists for any length of time with a strong push of water coming down for three or four weeks, then the period immediately after the normal level is reached will often see the pike start to feed ravenously. Back in January 1967 Ray was fishing a water that had been running high and coloured for six whole weeks, during which time the going had been rough. By the middle of the month the water fell rapidly away to normal level and immediately he was into a pike of 20½ lb taken on livebait. Only a mere starter this however, for over the following fortnight or so that stretch of water really produced the goods. Eleven fish over the twenty pound mark were taken and scores at lesser weights by a mere half a dozen anglers.

Such swims, which the pike stick to through thick and thin, may be truly described as pike lairs, and we have tried to distinguish at various places in this book between the methods needed to catch 'easy' pike, that is when they are *beginning* a big feeding spree, in their lairs, and methods needed to catch 'lazy' pike. Free-line livebaiting, ledgered livebaiting, and sparsely hooked static deadbaits are methods which succeed when things are dour, although they are perfectly good techniques even when the pike are moving well. However, as I implied at the beginning of the chapter there are less spectacular kinds of lairs occupied by one or more fish more or less permanently.

Newport Long Pond (Fig. 13) is a water in which we know the details of the whole of the fishable bank. Good pike swims were marked down, usually where the shallows sloped off quickly into relatively deep water and yet had fringing common reeds. One or two good pike were resident in the swims and one little 6-pounder was a regular to our landing net. It is in these swims, the pikes' lairs, that the pike anglers get those takes where the pike swallows the bait without moving. Several waters of my experience, Hornsea and Newport included, had these swallowing-on-the-spot pike long before they had seen many herrings. If the piker is unfortunate enough to get a pike swallow his hooks badly, and it is impossible to snip the hook to pieces, he should leave the hook in the fish and not attempt any tugging or pulling. That pike can live with a hook in it is indicated by the numbers of fish I have seen caught with anything up to four sets of trebles in their throats. Judging by the amount of monofil hanging out of their mouths these pike had won the battle in the manner most humiliating for the angler, namely, by snapping him. Bill Chillingsworth, Laurie Manns and I once fished a water where *one in four* of the fish caught had hooks and nylon in their mouths. On the other hand Ray and I found a 17½-pounder apparently killed by a huge treble hook in its throat. This fish had also broken its would-be captor: but I must say I have never before or since seen a treble hook as big as that one. To the serious angler, always attentive and thinking about his tackle, I do not think deep hooking remains a problem: certainly I do not think stationary deadbait as a method should be banned because it can be abused by the thoughtless. Whilst on the subject of deep hooking I would mention Dug Taylor's suggestion that would solve all problems: Dug thought of putting a single treble hook three inches up the trace above the deadbait's tail!

Fig. 26. Bill Giles' deadbait hooking arrangement using large trebles, and thick Alasticum single strand wire: the tackle is retrieved slowly using sink-and-draw system (see text).

There is one final hooking arrangement that I should like to mention (Fig. 26), and this is the system used by Bill Giles the renowned Norfolk pike specialist: one leading angling writer described it as all wrong, but since Bill has had over thirty 20-pound pike to this rig it cannot be all that wrong. It has been used with success in many waters, including hotspots (where I myself would not expect it to be very good when the fish were 'off'), and consists of two or three largish trebles tied to thick, single strand Alasticum wire. The herring is attached *facing the wrong way* according to the traditional methods, but the important point is that on the retrieve the deadbait comes in head first. Bill takes full advantage of this on the retrieve and really works it in carefully, and has, in fact, taken many big pike by doing this. As I say, there cannot be much wrong with a method used by one of the most successful pike anglers in Britain; he had his 57th birthday when out with us, and you can well imagine the years of experience and success that go to make up his present angling approach. Bill, in fact, was catching pike on herrings from Broadland hotspots when several famous anglers were saying that pike on the Broads would not take ledgered deadbaits.

Some strange things happen in hotspots. If you are unlucky enough to get snapped up you may find the pike reluctant to leave the company of its fellows. I had two very fluky captures under just such circumstances, having snapped on the strike when using a large perch as livebait. The line actually parted just on the stop knot so I must have pulled it a bit tight. After towing my float about for some time it decided, seemingly reluctantly, to leave the area and went off way over to the other side where it holed up close to the bank. Nothing much was happening so I reeled in to the bank my other rod which was baited with herring, fitted up a spinning rod, and set off on the half-mile walk in an attempt to tangle the spinner in the line being pulled around by the pike. When I finally arrived at the opposite point I found to my dismay that the 'lost' pike had gone back to the hotspot! At this point I began to think that fate had it in for me since although my deadbait rod had been reeled right in to the rod, the 'lost' pike swam round the deadbait line and began towing it across the water roughly in my direction. I waited and waited and sure enough in it came to the point it had visited on its first long wander. Eventually I was able to snag the lines with the spinner and began playing the fish very, very gently. Suddenly its strength increased enormously and I found myself playing two pike; the herring, which was being dragged along by the 'lost' pike, had itself been taken by a big fish. As I got them both closer to the bank the first fish managed to slide the line off the spinner, but I played in the 'herring' fish, and netted it shortly after: 17¾ lb. As 'jammy' a fish as you could ask for. I went after the first fish again, tangled the line with the spinner, just below the float, and Mick Griffiths finally netted it for me: 14½ lb. An angler cannot ask for much more than that in a day's fishing, yet I reckon I earned my luck. Anyway I got three more doubles that day.

And then we had the hobnail boot marks. This used to happen on the Hornsea Mere hotspot: no sign of a run and yet when the herring was drawn in it would have some squarish, or rectangular, dents just as though somebody wearing hobnail boots had stamped on it. This happened three or four times, and we never did solve it, but I like to think that my father, a non-angler, came up with the best answer: 'Nay lad, it's a pike so old and so big, that his teeth have been worn down to mere stumps.'

II

No need to search for a reason for the Hornsea hotspots of course; no shadow of doubt exists in my mind that the ever increasing boat traffic was responsible for pushing the pike up to the quieter reaches of the western end. If I had really thought about it the true facts of the situation should have occurred to me much earlier. The coots, moorhens, mallards, pheasants and birdlife generally, all were fully aware that beyond the boundary posts was a stretch of undisturbed water and they never ventured out into the fishable area. It should not have come as a surprise to me to find that the pike too were thinking along similar lines. Even the starlings knew they were on to a good thing, coming to roost from all over the area every evening just before dusk in the sanctuary, during the months before the really cold weather. In several other instances I have found congregations of birdlife on the surface matched by a shoal of pike underneath. It is one of the signs I look for these days when trying to form an idea about where the fish have gone. At sea, of course, one of the best ways to locate a shoal of bass is to find a flock of gulls hovering and wheeling around. Anglers have been well aware of this fact for many years and the position on our inland fisheries is not all that different.

For tight packing of really big pike the shoal in residence on a short stretch of the Barmston Drain in East Yorkshire some years ago takes some beating. Over a long period I had regularly crossed this shallow, narrow, uninviting-looking water. The species was present there of course, but specimen-sized fish seemed unlikely in the extreme. Imagine my surprise then, when only a matter of eight or nine years ago two 23-pounders were taken in double quick time. Before the season was ended two more 'twenties' were landed, one by a personal friend of mine, Bill Ellerker, who had been fishing Hornsea for years without ever topping the magical mark. His 'Barmy' capture went well over the mark weighing $22\frac{1}{4}$ lb. To very light pressure of angling this insignificant-looking drain had turned up four pike over 20 lb in one season, a good return this for many of our best-known fisheries, and enough to prompt me to ring up the local River Board official, Stan Metcalfe, for further information. 'Four 20-pounders from Barmston comes as no surprise to me,' said Stan. 'When we netted that same drain a mile or two farther upstream recently in a matter of a mere hundred yards of water we took fifteen 'twenties' and many at lesser weights putting them all into the tidal reaches of the River Hull'. What an astonishing congregation of big pike crammed into a short stretch of water; too bad I had just about finished my piking operations in that area. Had I been on to the hotspot several years previously I would have had some great days on this sluggish, tiny drain.

Marked baits too can sometimes put the discerning angler on to a shoal of pike for there are days when the bait, live or dead, is just picked up, crunched and rejected without further interference. One spot where I used to ledger livebaits regularly saw the roach come back with scales ripped off in numbers, often on one side only, even though there had been no sign of a run. Back again a few days later, however, four or five takes would often occur in a couple of hours or so. This sort of sport happened so frequently that it quickly became obvious that I had dropped on one of the very best swims in the whole of the fishery. This hotspot did in fact provide me with some of my most memorable days.

CHAPTER 13

PIKE FROM BOATS

Ray Webb

With my early piking being done in Lincolnshire it was, in consequence, almost invariably practised from the bank. Without ever really thinking about it one automatically fell into line with the approach generally in use. In three or four winters of intensive effort practically every other angler I saw out and about went into action on foot. My regular angling companions at that time did likewise, so it is hardly surprising that I did not in those early years, get round to seriously considering the possibilities of tackling the fish from a boat. In the early sixties however after the fashion of so many other pike enthusiasts at that time I made a number of trips down to Norfolk in search of the outsize specimens that were being taken so regularly from the waters of the Upper Thurne, and this inevitably meant a switch to boat fishing. It just was not done in that part of the world to set out for a day's fishing unless you had a boat available.

Setting the trend of course was the big name of the area, Dennis Pye, a confirmed boat angler and familiar figure in his inevitable peaked cap with a large Alsatian dog as his only companion. The preceding top man too, Jim Vincent, famous amongst other things for the 5 in spoon which bears his name, was also in the habit of doing his pike fishing from a boat. So acting on the axiom of 'When in Rome do as the Romans do', I also went afloat out from Martham, up Candle Dyke and on to the two miles of shallow, clear, reed-fringed water that was Hickling Broad. Initially I found the new style far from easy to take to, the old approach from the bank being much more to my liking, but by sticking to the task, gradually confidence and enthusiasm grew until I reached the point where it was obvious that a vast amount of boat fishing lay ahead of me. At this stage I set about making one of my own, a decision I have never had cause to regret. The pleasure derived from building and using the old tub far outweighed the time and effort involved in its construction. Technically and theoretically speaking, it may not be so hot, since it was not so much designed as evolved. It was added to in bits and pieces over the years, after having started life as a seven and a half feet punt for small pond work. In spite of a number of imperfections, I am now able to tackle the larger Irish loughs, some of them twenty miles or so in length, and can cope single-handed with the unloading from the roof of my van, launching, and vice-versa. It can surely be truthfully claimed to have justified its existence.

Having spent so much of my angling time over the last ten years afloat in a considerable variety of crafts, for it has not always been possible, or even desirable, to operate from my own in every circumstance, it has been easy for me to form a comprehensive idea of the advantages and disadvantages of boat angling, the situation where it so frequently wins hand down and the occasional one where it does not. Perhaps the first advantage to being afloat that became obvious immediately when I started fishing the Norfolk Broads, was the fact that it opened up so much water that would otherwise have been inaccessible because of excessive casting distances. Banks that were waterlogged, boggy, or fringed by a fifteen-yard margin of reeds two or three feet high, or in many cases festooned with 'Private Keep Out' notices, that made any approach from the landward side extremely hazardous were now within my reach. In those days the method in favour was livebaiting fished intensively in one spot for a mere twenty minutes or so then up anchoring and on to another swim. By doing this a considerable area of water was covered in a day's fishing. This of course was the style adopted and publicized by Dennis Pye. His tremendous returns put him way out ahead in the history of pike fishing and absolutely in a class of his own. They were, however, only possible by tackling the waters involved from a boat; without one he could not have hoped for comparable results. Another point where the boat proved its worth was in the matter of studying the water, looking for likely swims prior to going out with the tackle set up for a serious attempt to catch fish. So much of the most promising water of the Upper Thurne area being clear and shallow it was a common practice of Pye and others to spend a considerable amount of time quietly drifting the boat along keeping an eye out for likely spots. Very often the pike themselves were spotted and the position carefully noted in readiness for the time when angling in earnest would begin. I myself on many occasions in the close season, have launched the old boat, Tinca by name after my other great favourite species, the Tench, and have taken pencil and paper aboard and spent countless hours compiling maps showing depth contours, weed beds, snags, variations in the nature of the bottom etc. so recording information that has come in handy time and again; often long after the survey was carried out and the information obtained forgotten. Virtually all my work in this field however was carried out in water of far greater depth and colour than that of the Upper Thurne, so the job was done by employing a heavy weight attached to a long cord, sounding the bottom in this fashion, much the same as the naval men have done for centuries, swinging the lead to guide their boats safely over shallow water. Pye of course is strictly a livebaiting man, but Jim Vincent preferred to employ a 5 in spoon, a method where the regular casting and retrieving involved inevitably means getting snagged up with some frequency, far more so perhaps than with any other technique, and if operating on foot from the bank heavy tackle losses can become an expensive item. Out in a boat, however, the chances of recovering hooked-up baits are greatly improved; by moving directly over the snag and employing a gaff in shallow water or some sort of drag on a stout cord in the deeps, the tackle plus the obstruction itself can on many occasions be hauled up to the surface. Very often by working in this fashion I have not only retrieved my own bait but also a bonus in the shape of other lines, swivels, anti-kink vanes and fold-over leads. Some of the more formidable obstacles, if in a heavily fished location can yield a bumper harvest—and a very rich and worthwhile harvest in these inflationary times, for the price of pike baits has soared in recent years, as indeed have all costs of equipment. Another point where the man in the boat scores heavily if spinning in clear water, is in his ability to actually see his bait working from the moment it hits the water. He is able to observe its action, the depth at which it is operating, and the amount of flash it is emitting. By being able to work in close to the pike and fish a fairly short line all these things can be observed visually whereas the bank angler, usually having to go in for extreme distance casting, can only work by the feel of his tackle, a far less effective method of operation. It is surprising how some spoons fish with a lively action in flowing water but when transferred to a lake come in completely dead, needing considerable modification with a pair of pliers before they are working satisfactorily. One of the greatest thrills of all in pike fishing is to actually see the fish dart out and take the lure, as can frequently happen when afloat. I remember vividly one occasion, when after casting and retrieving a four-inch blue and silver spoon time and time again through four feet of clear, fast-running water without any sign of response, suddenly, just as the bait was under the rod tip and about to be lifted clear of the surface, a huge shape materialized, moved to the bait with astonishing rapidity, just about drowned me with spray as it turned to race away up and across the stream, and fought with tremendous power for some considerable time before finishing up in the net. For sheer, breathtaking impact this style of fishing is in a class of its own.

There is more to it than mere enjoyment. By watching the take, making note of where the pike came from, what depth it took at, which way it went on being hooked and how it actually grabbed the lure in its mouth it is possible to gain a lot of information which will prove of value. By moving the boat over to the spot where the fish came from for instance a close inspection will often, after a number of captures have been made, see a pattern emerging as to the type of swim to look for so improving one's knowledge and prospects for future sport. One such examination after the taking of a superb pike of $28\frac{1}{4}$ lb caused me some astonishment for the fish had been lying quietly in a mere eighteen inches of water completely unperturbed by my drifting downstream to within ten yards of it before lowering the anchor, admittedly as quietly as possible, and then commencing casting and retrieving. Only two or three casts were made when the pike struck, missed, struck again, successfully this time and surged away downstream on the longest run I ever experienced with any fish. There must have been seventy or eighty yards of line ripped off the spool in double quick time before I succeeded in halting the initial rush. The fight continued at extreme long range for what seemed an eternity but was I suppose in fact some ten minutes long. From that day on I have never written off even the shal-

lowest water as being incapable of holding outsize specimens, but
thinking it over, the river was running high, fast and coloured at
the time. It was in fact just fining down after a flood otherwise
perhaps a pike of this weight would hardly have been taken from
quite so close to the bank. Over in Ireland on the big loughs,
trolling is the method usually employed and for this of course a
boat is essential. The idea is to cruise along with the outboard
working at a slow tick-over speed, the bait fishing way out behind,
often at the end of fifty or sixty yards of line. This method is
often criticized as being the most boring of all, it certainly seems
that way sometimes when there is nothing doing. On a day
when fish are in taking mood however there is little danger of
anyone dozing off, believe me.

There are two sides to most questions of course and this one
is no exception, the unquestionably noisier approach by boat
tending to discourage many anglers, but though some pike may
perhaps be inclined to move away as a boat draws near I can
quote from my own experience plenty of instances where they
did not. Way back in 1963 out afloat on Hornsea with Tag Barnes
and Johnny Neville a discussion developed on this very topic
early on in the day, to be forgotten entirely as the pike came on
feed at dusk. Tag latched into a fish that skipped about in lively
fashion for some time with myself standing up armed with a gaff
and John as usual issuing instructions right left and centre
about how the job should be done. With all this commotion
going on the boat was rocking to an alarming degree, but even
so, with all three of us on our feet making little or no attempt to
conceal ourselves, another pike sneaked right in under the stern,
picked up a herring that had accidentally dropped over the side
some time previously and sauntered casually away obviously in
no way alarmed by our antics. About this time too, afloat on
Grimsthorpe Lake near Grantham once again with John as my
companion, a run developed to ledgered herring so I reeled in
the other rod with livebait attached and laid it just out over the
side. Tightening rapidly on to the taking fish, contact was made
only for a few brief seconds before the hooks pulled clear, yet
while retrieving the mangled bait with some disgust I was
astonished to see the livebait rod bent double, just about to slip
out into the lake. In fact a fish of some five pounds or so had
come in close and calmly snaffled the bait while I had been busy

attending to the other rod. Time and again I have come across pike of all sizes, small, medium and colossal, that have fed confidently so close in that they must almost have been touching the side of the boat. It has happened so often that I have few worries these days about them taking alarm if I decide to go afloat for the day instead of working along the bank on foot. One point where the boat angler is at a disadvantage however is when it comes to netting or gaffing a beaten fish, especially is this so in fast-running water. With the powerful current surging along as the tiring pike comes to the surface downstream of the boat it tends to start revolving rapidly, a terrifying procedure when only one small treble serves to maintain contact between the angler and his quarry. If the pike can be worked up above the angler's position he can, if employing a large net, release the pressure and scoop up the beaten fish as it is swept rapidly downstream. It is a chancy business at the best and completely impractical with a gaff. When the pike in question is really big it may be a physical impossibility to boat the fish at all as I found out on one occasion when the push of water downstream on the exhausted fish was sufficient to cancel out the maximum pull I was able to exert in an upstream direction. The fish held steady some ten yards below the boat; truly a nightmare situation if ever there was one. Only one thing was possible as far as I could see and that was to up-anchor the boat, drift to the bank where the current was not so powerful and use the landing net. The scheme worked out admirably in practice, but had I hooked that fish from the bank the problem would never have arisen in the first place.

Probably the biggest drawback of all to boat fishing is the danger involved especially on the larger waters. In spite of all the warnings every year sees a number of fatal accidents many of which could and should have been prevented had a more thoughtful approach to the problem been adopted. Even the ability to swim can often be more of a hindrance than a help for in cold, rough, wintry weather so much heavy clothing is needed to keep warm and dry that a strong swimmer would soon find himself in difficulties if pitched over the side without some form of lifesaving equipment. The drag of waterlogged gear and the numbing effect of icy cold water are enough to beat the best of swimmers in a surprisingly short time. The danger is reduced if

PLATE 13
$31\frac{1}{2}$ lb to static ledgered mackerel head. The end of a long road for Barrie.

PLATE 14

24¼ lb. from Horsey Mere. Tackle: ledgered herring.

one has a companion aboard but even then teamwork and co-operation are essential in a small boat if disaster is to be averted. I well remember one Christmas on the Norfolk Broads some years ago, moored to the bank of a small cutting fishing hard to

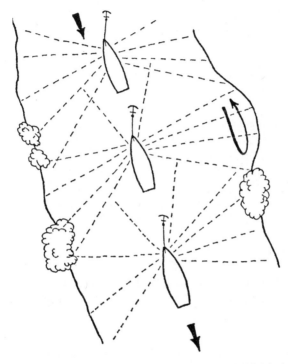

Fig. 27. Ray's method of covering the water with artificials by drifting downstream in stages. At each anchor position a variety of lures is tried. Black arrows indicate direction of current.

obtain a supply of livebait for a day's piking. I stood up in the boat with my companion Bob Ranby operating from the bank. With a good supply of roach in the net I decided that one last cast would be enough but unbeknown to me Bob had quit fishing already and had started to climb aboard. After a bitter cold night there was a considerable amount of ice about and Bob lost his footing and fell lengthways along the gunwale, his sixteen and a half stones being more than enough to capsize the seven feet seven inch Gremlin dinghy. I somersaulted neatly into the air executing as neat a jack-knife entry into the water as one could ever hope to see; Bob too took to the water but fortunately we were both able to scramble out quickly and suffered no ill effects except the loss of a day's piking which was plenty bad enough for me. The incident did however drive home most forcibly the lesson that teamwork is essential if two or more anglers are afloat at the same time in a small boat so some benefit at least was derived from the day's disaster.

Whether one likes it or not the trend is obviously towards more and more boat fishing. An ever-increasing number of anglers seem to be owning their own boats these days with modern fibreglass-constructed hulls tending to oust the old clinker-built jobs, and outboard motors taking the work out of it all making a pair of oars of mere auxiliary value as you might say. Personally I prefer to row wherever possible but with everybody else churning the water up with four, five and six horse power engines going full blast it is sheer futility to suppose to try and effect a noiseless approach—though I still feel inclined to make the effort. There are, of course times, and places, when boat fishing scores and others when it is better to base one's operations on the bank, but beyond all doubt a man has to be able to cope confidently with the problems imposed by going afloat after the fish before he can ever hope to call himself a complete angler.

II

Like Ray I was pitched into boat fishing for pike by force of circumstances, firstly on Hornsea Mere where the bank fishing is very restricted, and later, much more intensively, on the Irish loughs. Christine and I spent a couple of years in Eire, and most of our fishing was done from a seventeen feet, clinker-built Shannon longboat. It is difficult to imagine a craft better built for trolling (or trailing, as some people insist) the vastness of Lough Ree. These craft are easily handled by one person on the oars even in quite rough conditions, and I used to troll by rowing and leaning the rod over the stern then either keeping the rod handle button under my toe end, or jamming it under a special piece of wood. On getting a take the rod tip usually dips savagely down:

a strike is almost always unnecessary, but it *is* critical to dig the oars deep into the water to stop the boat quickly.

When trolling the margins or under rough conditions an angler alone in the boat is always in difficulties, and it is often more by luck than judgement that the pike ends up in the boat, particularly when one is a beginner at the task. I have always tended to use lines of 12–15 lb breaking strain and a ten foot Farstrike carp rod for trolling, but the Irish technique of using approximately 30 lb breaking strain line and shorter, stiffer rods may well be the better method for the angler who habitually trolls alone.

Using this stronger gear it is a much simpler matter to stop the boat—less risk of breakage anyway—and to turn the bows away from the margins before playing the fish properly. With luck it may even be possible to drop the anchor if the wind conditions tend to blow the craft into the reeds. It can be imagined that every move has to be worked out in advance: the position of every item in the boat must be known; all nets, gaffs, anchors and so on must be easily to hand.

If an outboard is used for trolling it is an easy matter to turn the bows in the right direction when a pike takes. It is also possible to fish by holding the rod and actually feeling for the take, a method which allows one to take one's eyes off the rod tip and watch where the craft is going! Under all except calm and sunlit conditions I've always been very happy about trolling on the outboard. Dave Cumpstone loaned me a four horse-power job, the name of which I cannot recall, and by keeping it just ticking over I could fish very much closer to the reedy margins than when trolling on the oars. There is also a constancy about the outboard which makes for pleasant and comfortable fishing.

However, by far the most efficient way of trolling lures is to have two or three anglers in the boat, one taking care of the oars or the outboard and the other one or two actually fishing. Christine and I used to take twenty-minute spells on the oars, except when she was pregnant when the arrangement was for Christine to hook the fish and then hand the rod over to me. We took some splendid, hard-battling pike on Lough Ree, the best going 25¼ lb to a seven inch, silver Jim Vincent-like spoon, and a fish which still ranks as Christine's best. Ray's best fish also fell to spoon on an Irish lough, and I remain the odd one out by taking my best pike on suspended deadbait on an English river.

There are other ways of piking from a boat than by trolling of course, though let it be firmly said, as my last word on the subject, that trolling is more often hectic than boring. I think those that have been bored have probably picked the brightest, sunniest days to go afloat, a reasonable temptation to which to succumb, if the least likely to succeed. One of the most enjoyable methods of piking from the boat is to gently search the margins and bays, on the oars, and cast plugs or spinners into likely looking shallows. The ideal sort of spot often has thinly spread common reed stems in several feet of water. This kind of swim can often be searched with a livebait; a technique widely used on the Broads and popularized by Dennis Pye.

When one considers the more static methods of fishing, such as stationary deadbaiting, activity in the boat has to be curtailed to a minimum. As Ray says, it is quite amazing how close pike will approach to a boat; this is true also of trolling and Christine and I took almost all our fish on lures fished a mere five to ten yards behind the boat. However, I do not believe in taking chances: always wear soft shoes when afloat, and make a great effort to avoid dropping tins on the bottom boards. Some people are incapable of sitting still in a boat, no matter how large, but on the other hand it must be admitted that few boat seats are comfortable. I have yet to see a well-designed angler's boat, and the only suggestion I can make to increase comfort is to take aboard a basket or chair, if this is possible, and plenty of foam cushions. Most fishing boats used in England are too small, and it is rarely possible to crouch in the bottom out of the way of easterly winds. We could also do with some well designed boat 'rod rests'. Almost every boat angler I meet has his own ideas about what these should be, and the best I have come up with for trolling or stationary deadbait fishing is to lay a cloth over the gunwale to hold the rod still and stop the rod varnish chipping. A bit primitive I agree.

I am in the process of buying another boat, having sold my big Shannon boat when I came back to Cambridge. I enjoyed the clinker-built job, and even enjoyed renovating it under Fred Carter's expert eye—Fred Carter of Garnafailagh fame. But, my word, they certainly need some upkeeping. I suspect a smaller fibreglass craft will be less beautiful to manage in the water. What spare time I have, however, goes into fishing and not into boat building and so serviceability will have to be the keynote in future ventures. There are so many occasions when a boat is useful, if not for fishing then for exploration of waters, that I shall not be long before replacing the Shannon boat.

CHAPTER 14

IRISH PIKING

Ray Webb

With an international reputation for the wealth of its pike fishing
Ireland automatically becomes the Mecca for all anglers who
have any interest in the species at all, at least one holiday over
there every year being an absolute must. Men who have done
consistently well on English pike fisheries for a number of years
set off convinced that they must inevitably break all records
once they are let loose on the Irish waters but it so often works
out in practice that they return home somewhat soured and
disillusioned having done far, far worse over there than if they'd
stayed at home. It is not just a case of novice or average anglers
failing to produce the expected results, either, for some of our
best pike men have made the trip only to return beaten, wondering
exactly how and where they went wrong. Just what is it then
about the Irish pike fishing that has our men floundering about
so, all at sea, completely unable to come to terms with the
situation? Having myself succeeded, and failed too come to that,
on both sides of the Irish Sea I am well placed to view the position from all angles and come up with some, if not all, of the
answers to the problem.

Probably the most obvious and important difference between
the pike fishing in both countries is in the sheer size of the waters
involved. So many of Ireland's best fisheries are of absolutely
tremendous expanse. Twenty miles or more in length by five
miles or so wide, such colossal sheets of water have to be actually
visited and seen by the English angler before he can get anything
like a true picture in his mind. One of our better known pike
men, on catching his first glimpse of Lough Allen gasped,
obviously taken aback, muttering something about 'Only a
loony would tackle a water of that size; have you anything in
the way of fisheries some half a mile or so in length?' Such a

reaction is quite commonplace and understandable, yet Lough Allen is only a fair to middling stretch of water by Irish standards being in fact eight miles in length.

When faced with a lake of these sort of proportions the visitor is of course often at a loss as to where to make a start, his first move as outlined in Chapter 11 is obviously to seek local knowledge and in this respect the position in Ireland is usually far superior to that of obtaining it in this country. To assist the tourists Ireland is divided into zones and each major angling centre has its own Development Association with a secretary at the helm. Whenever I have wandered into a district for the first time my initial move has always been to look up this extremely hard-working official and a very wise decision this invariably proves to be. I often wonder if these chaps are all sent to a training school somewhere. Whether that is in fact so or not you can bet your bottom dollar this local secretary will definitely be the right man for the job. Coming back to Lough Allen for instance, half an hour spent with Senator Joseph Mooney will clearly illustrate my point. He will bring out a scrapbook full of cuttings that will provide all the information required to make a start.

Depths of course are all important on these bigger lakes. One hundred and fifty feet or more can frequently be found. Such areas can be ruled out straight away as barren and infertile. Irish waters generally however, are much clearer than the English fisheries, being in the main pollution free, and weed-growth flourishes, as a consequence, down to a considerably greater depth. Lily pads, for example, can often be found on Lough Ree with long thin stems growing up from the bottom all the way to the surface some twelve or fourteen feet away. It is hardly surprising that the pike over there seem to live at somewhat greater depths than is usually the case in this country. Twenty-five to thirty feet of water will regularly yield good returns whilst the shallows around the fringes fail completely. One local bit of advice being to fish where the dark water begins, meaning at the point where the bottom is lost from sight and this usually happens at around the twenty feet mark. To fully understand the meaning of the term gin-clear water, a trip to Lough Corrib is advised. On a clear day even the tiniest pebble can be seen on the bottom some twenty-five feet or more down, yet fishless though the water would seem to be, pike will appear from nowhere in a flash to intercept a correctly worked bait, such is the camouflage that nature provides. Pike can on occasions be taken from shallow water but nothing like so regularly as the English angler would expect when fishing through the summer months with the temperature well up. Bob Reynolds and Fred Wagstaffe found this out on Templehouse Lough in September 1969. For several days they flogged the weedy shallows of four or five feet in depth, a policy fully in accordance with all the accepted teachings on their home waters, but nothing of note was produced until they switched their attentions to eighteen feet of water at which point contact was made with the really big stuff.

Weedbeds too will repay investigation. A boat anchored fifteen yards or so away will allow the angler to work his bait along the edges of the growth, a really determined tug-of-war being required to pull the fish into clear water in the event of a take. Strange as it may seem to us, however, the Irish anglers tend to leave this sort of water unfished, not that they are unaware of its fish-holding potential, it is just that they class it unsuitable for trolling. This is the only method they seem to have any time for. On Lough Ree in June 1970 all my enquiries yielded the same instructions. Find a rough rocky bottom where the shallows drop away into deeper water, no one showing any interest in the weedy stretches at all. Beyond all doubt pike do lie up amongst the rocks but unfortunately the depth varies so quickly under a boat moving smartly along with a bait being trolled some fifty yards or so behind, one minute the depth is reading at a steady thirty feet, the next it shelves up rapidly to a mere eighteen inches or less. When one has seen the size and cutting edges of some of the boulders strewn about all over Lough Ree this sudden depth variation can be disconcerting in the extreme, especially so in times of rough weather when the sight of an enormous jaggy rock peeping up through the trough of a wave as one's boat is sliding rapidly down off the crest can so easily turn the English angler to thinking wistfully of the tiny farmyard duckpond full of pike back in his home country. As one chap, very much a landlubber, put it to me, 'Better by far to stick to my local drains and pits. They might not offer the same chance of a 30-pounder but at least I shall live to tell the tale.' The water just off from the shores of an island is also often recommended as worth a trial and my own experience bears this out to be true. On some Irish loughs, no matter how large, one is sometimes tempted to think that there is really no option but to be fishing round some island or other; they are literally dotted about here, there and everywhere. The story has it that on lower Lough Erne there are three hundred and sixty-five of them, one for every day of the year. Having been out on the water at various points of its twenty miles or so of length I can well believe that this is so.

Having come to some sort of conclusion as to where the pike are likely to be the next thing for the visiting angler to decide is how to get them out. For a start he must realize that, in spite of having been brought up to begin piking on October 1st and continue through the colder months until March 14th, his fishing in Ireland will have to be adapted to and carried out in the summertime for it is true beyond all doubt that so many of Ireland's best fisheries go completely dead after the first real frost. It is often put forward, by way of explanation, that the pike, with a water temperature rapidly falling to its winter level, retreat into the really deep water, going into a state of hibernation and there could well be something in this. Right or wrong, and there are other theories proffered, winter fishing is best forgotten, September being plenty late enough in the year to book a holiday in Ireland with pike in mind. In my opinion it is warm weather piking all the way, with April seeing the very best of it on many waters. From acceptance of this seasonal difference the next move is to settle on a technique to use and this, if he follows the local custom will inevitably mean the visitor turning to trolling, a method that he is highly unlikely ever to have seen used on his home waters.

It is all boat work, of course, and the outboard is rapidly ousting the oars as a means of propulsion, the usual idea being to run the engine at as slow a tick-over speed as possible, play out fifty yards of line or more terminating in a wire trace and a spoon three to six inches in length. The boat is taken through likely pike-holding water several times before moving on to cover a different area. In this fashion literally miles of water can be, and usually are, tried at least once during the course of a day's fishing, but after a few days' work a number of spots where the pike can be said to be congregated will become apparent to the discerning angler. Once this is so these hot swims need to be accurately located by taking a line or two from marking points on the land. On such vast sheets of water the fish will be lost as soon as they are found unless this is done, distances over water being very deceptive indeed. It was on my first visit to Lough Mask that I had this lesson so forcibly brought home to me. What appeared as a short journey of about a mile did in fact turn out to be rather more than three times that distance. One item of equipment that might on first thoughts be considered superfluous when this style of fishing is being employed, is a heavy holding anchor on a rope of some length. When a pike is hooked, especially in rough weather, the boat tends to drift along at an alarming rate once the outboard is switched off, towing the finally exhausted fish several yards away in its wake. With the anchor down and the boat holding steady on a long length of rope the problem is eased considerably. There is only, in this case, the vertical up and down motion of the craft to contend with though this in itself can well be enough for most. I have hauled pike aboard myself on a number of occasions working from the crouch position being loath to stand up straight for fear of being toppled over the side. Alternatively a beaten fish can be towed slowly along into calmer more sheltered waters provided any is available within reasonable range, this being the practice regularly adopted by the Irish anglers as I have seen for myself on a number of occasions. For many visiting English anglers however, the trolling technique will prove difficult to take to. I myself do not care to employ it unless absolutely necessary but fortunately as previously indicated, a bait fished by casting and retrieving from a stationary boat will often prove just as effective, even more so at times. Less water is covered of course so an informed estimate of the pike's where-abouts is needed to offset this. An extensive sheltering weedbed is one of the obvious spots to try. Depths of up to fifteen feet or so can yield outstanding results to this method, but above this figure returns usually decline rapidly, probably the bait tends to be coming back to the boat at too steep an angle. There is the added advantage when employing this method around a weed-bed of tackling water that is rarely if ever fished by the per-petually trolling Irish anglers. It was from such a spot some ten to eleven feet deep on Lough Ree that I took a 29 lb pike in July 1970, the closest I have come to a 30-pounder yet. Equally gratifying perhaps was the second big one of 28¼ lb boated just a few short weeks later again to the same technique. Here two twenties plus a long list of 'doubles' being proof that the visiting angler does not necessarily have to troll if the method is not to his liking.

In addition to trying the pike with artificials there are times and places where an intelligently worked livebait will yield results in Ireland though one's choice of bait is somewhat restricted, perch and rudd being the only two species available in most areas. Once again only a very limited amount of water is covered in a day compared with the trolling man's vast mileage. He is virtually bound to present his bait to a pike or two somewhere along the way whereas a livebaiter, on a water of some twenty miles or so in length, can quite easily miss the pike completely all the way from dawn to dusk. A quick switch to livebaiting once the pike have been located on the troll can work out extremely well at times, the combination of methods yielding better results than would have been likely to either technique employed individually. Over on the River Shannon I watched an angler from Leeds trot a 4 oz perch downstream to a pike that had just rolled on the surface to take a fish straightaway that missed the 20 lb mark by ounces only. Dennis Pye has taken good double-figure fish in Ireland by his favourite method. Tried more regularly I am firmly convinced that livebaiting would yield results consistently on a number of waters but it will be left to the visiting English angler to put the matter to the test; for the local man it is very much a case of trolling or nothing at all.

The prospects for the ledgered deadbait enthusiast are at the moment extremely difficult to assess, so little having been done in this direction. One of the problems, not met with in England, is the procuring of baits, herrings and mackerel being available only on rare occasions at many angling centres. Odd pikes are reported in the angling press to ledgered deadbait used on Irish waters so there must be some sort of prospect good, bad or indifferent. My somewhat limited attempts on Lough Ree using a dead perch failed to produce any runs and Fred Carter, the well-known angler and guest-house owner of Garnafailagh, once left a deadbait out on a line with no hooks attached for six weeks just to see if it was taken but once again there was nothing doing. Some of the Irish waters look ideal for the use of the method. They have weed- and snag-free bottoms but as with livebaiting it is going to take a number of pioneer deadbait enthusiasts from England to put in a lot of time and effort before the potential becomes apparent.

Such then are some of the problems awaiting and the answers needed by the angler visiting Ireland for the first time. Just how far he will succeed depends to a large extent on his early realization of the differences involved between this and his native fishing and his ability to adapt his approach accordingly. Failure to make the necessary changes will, I am afraid, almost inevitably see him returning home convinced that the Irish piking is grossly overrated. This I know for a fact is not so, tackled along the right lines. The waters of the Emerald Isle will yield as good if not better, returns than are to be found anywhere on earth in settings that are as glorious and peaceful as could ever be wished for.

II

Here writes another Irish piking failure; to begin with anyway. Whilst the English pike angler can use the same rods, reels, lines and artificial baits in Eire, it pays to forget all he has learnt in England and seek local advice. I would agree that information given in Eire is usually better than one can obtain at home, with one proviso, and that is that to the Irishman any pike is a big pike. And any pike is too big to live with trout. Fortunately a great many Irish waters, even small ones, have some big pike in them, and though your informant may never have seen one bigger than four or five pounds, the chances are that you will do better.

Big loughs should be broken down into more manageable proportions. Find the best local trolling man and see if he will disclose the best stretches to you. Often he will do so, particularly if you invite him out for the day, or hire a boat from him. Often the really good stretches have nothing to identify them that cannot be found in dozens of places, and yet they and they alone hold the pike. Vast areas of these loughs hold few fish, and the hotspots can remain year after year unless they get hammered to death. Reedy margins always hold fish but usually small ones, only certain stretches holding anything like a head of big pike. As with off-shore marks they are best sorted out by trolling, and to some extent by spinning. Having found them the angler can begin to think about other methods such as live and deadbaiting. I wish him luck!

When Christine and I located one good hotspot by trolling, we switched over to livebaiting with $\frac{1}{2}-\frac{3}{4}$ lb rudd, and 6-8 oz perch, and failed to get a run of any kind. Deadbait spinning and deadbait trolling using perch, rudd, herring and mackerel also failed to produce any takes. Back to trolled 7 in spoon in the same swims produced a double-figure fish first time through the swim. In this particular hotspot the same result was obtained all the time we fished it, and to other good stretches on the Lough Ree system.

I have never been very good at acting upon advice given, although I do make a note of it, usually. In Ireland I was told to troll, and forget about livebaiting and deadbaiting, so naturally I did more of the latter first. I finished up trolling with big spoons. This raises another point: it pays to think big when using artificials in Irish loughs. I well remember Jimmy Ure using home-made spinners about 18 in long, each armed with treble hooks hanging from it like washing on a line, and catching pike too, down to fish of 3 lb.

Those great deep areas in excess of hundred feet are probably not entirely barren. For a start they are probably populated with Lough Ree monsters and the like. Apart from these, however, I remember Dave Cumpstone taking $\frac{1}{2}$ lb perch on lobworm from eighty feet down, and certainly eels are there too. Dave also picked up patches of living weed, although whether they grow there or had drifted in we never ascertained. Absolutely theoretically we decided that the giant pike of these loughs moved to the depths in winter, and we even worked out methods of getting to grips with them. Large deadbaits fished 'on the drift' under relatively calm conditions seemed a good idea. Possibly even deep-fished bream livebaits might succeed, for bream are happy at great depths. We even bought a very large shark float to carry out the tests, but for various reasons never got around to it. Any fishing of the great depths would require, it seems to me, relatively calm conditions, and anchoring would presumably be out of the question. It is a pretty problem, for on growth rate studies alone there must be many more 30 lb plus pike in, for example Lough Ree than are actually caught either on rod and line or by professional fishermen.

I think, also, that I would try eels at depth as live and dead-baits for pike love eels, and of course many anglers have suggested using eels as bait. Thinking back to my sea-fishing days we had no trouble at all with tangling, provided the bait was lip-hooked. I do not remember using eels larger than a few ounces however, and as far as pike are concerned I was thinking of baits in the half-pound category. I managed to get hold of a dead 2 lb eel recently and using the tail end, about 9 in of it, lying on the bottom, had a take within half an hour—a very rapid run which dropped it almost immediately. I still have not used my black rubber sandeel but intend to give it a good trial shortly. As a matter of fact my interest in small eels as livebait has never been concerned with fishing in normal waters where it is difficult to beat a good 6 oz 'slimy', but rather it has always been with the vast Irish loughs such as Ree and Derg, and the deeps they contain.

Our arguments for placing 30 lb plus pike in the depths in winter are long and complicated, but they go something like this. Firstly, the Irish pikers (trollers, or if you must be pedantic, trailers) certainly catch a good number of pike in excess of twenty pounds. These fish are taken, along with numbers of other doubles, in relatively shallow water at all times of year except in the depths of winter (November to February) when the Irish piker more or less gives up the ghost. My own experience in these hotspots is that the Irishmen know best, and that artificials (large wobbling spoons) really are superior to livebaits and deadbaits.

But the growth rate of pike on Lough Ree is very high, much higher than for Broads' fish for example, and so there ought to be large numbers of fish in excess of thirty pounds. When you consider that Ree is fished quite heavily for pike, and by good local anglers, it is surprising that only a few fish over thirty pounds have ever been taken, the best I think was 38 lb caught a few years ago by a chap spinning for trout with a trout-sized minnow.

Two conclusions can be drawn: either the giant pike are in the stretches not normally fished or else they are being killed whilst in their prime of life. The only parts of Lough Ree not often fished are the deeps. The reason is not hard to find: it is exceedingly difficult to troll effectively in one hundred feet of water—difficult to know where your bait is, how it is working, whether you have enough line out, and at the same time keep control of the craft in the often rough conditions. When I have tried it myself I just managed to cope after a fashion, but was never really confident that I was fishing properly. The only alternative is to fish in calm conditions, preferably during the early morning or evening.

Anchorage in the deeps is difficult and probably not wise. After all the rope will be going down quite steeply and there will be a good chance of big fish fouling it. Almost all techniques could be used with the boat drifting freely. A large deadbait can be fished almost stationary, or by sink and draw techniques or alternatively a livebait can be fished under a large sliding float. Trolling is carried out normally, but using the oars, not the outboard motor.

Of the three possibilities I fancy livebaiting, and here the problem of choice of bait arises. A good-sized bream would almost certainly be a good choice, but perhaps better, as I said above would be an eel, perhaps around the two-pound mark. Eels certainly inhabit the depths in numbers as well as the shallower reaches, and I should think form a high proportion of the pike's diet.

That then is the theoretical side of the where and how of Lough Ree's giant pike. My own fishing in such waters will now be restricted to holiday ventures, whereas Dave is at present living on the spot. And I hope, as I write, that he has already got to grips with the giants.

I said earlier that the giant pike may not exist in numbers because they were being culled at some stage. Fred Wagstaffe wrote an article in the magazine *Fishing* recently in which he mentioned the slaughter of pike on Lough Ree. I know that this slaughter exists. One weekend in 1967, one hundred and eighty-four good pike were killed by anglers on one day. If you are a pike, once you are caught on some Irish loughs that is the end— no second chance, no chance to learn or to grow. When you consider that pike are not spread evenly throughout a water, and that there are definite hotspots it may well be that the bulk of the pike population never gets a chance to reach old age. Personally I do not think this is too far fetched an idea even for a lough of sixteen miles in length. The anglers round that shore know where the hotspots are, and they fish them well. But certainly there are giants in these loughs, in spite of any reduction in numbers.

Well, that is one way of culling the big pike population. There

is another way. The Lough Ree monster. For years I have
laughed at these tales, whether they came second-hand to Fred
Carter at Garnafailagh, whether three Irish priests saw something
on the western shore, or whether the tales came from other
loughs than Ree and other countries than the Irish Republic.
Ray will confirm that I have always had the scientists' utter and
healthy (or unhealthy) scepticism: I laughed at F. W. Holliday's
fears, and Jimmy McM. Ure's tales of Ree. Apologies to all, for I
will not be laughing again, bejabbers. On the very week that Fred
Wagstaffe and party were flogging the lake for pike, Hugh
Reynolds and I were bream and tench fishing at the southern end
in the River Shannon, and in Killinure Lough. Whilst returning
from the Shannon at six o'clock in the morning on a clear and
glassy calm morning we saw something in shallowish water near
Hare Island that made us hightail it for home as fast as the
four horse-power outboard would go. We have already dis-
graced ourselves in Cambridge angling circles with our tale, and
lost the respect of a lot of angling friends into the bargain, so we
will not be repeating the details here. But I will not be all that
easy in my mind when I drift over the black deeps, in the gathering dusk, with a large deadbait, or a sizeable livebait working at
one hundred feet plus.

Coming back to earth a little I would like to conclude this
chapter with a tale that indicates there is great scope for experiment with artificials. Sharkbait Robbo of Chapter 7 fame once
gave me a huge pile of Norwegian spinners as a birthday present.
Amongst them was a 7 in concavo–convex silver wobbler. It
looked quite nice in the water but I never took a single pike on it
either in England or Ireland until, acting on the advice of a local,
I took a bankside rock and beat the hell out of it so that the
concavo–convex effect was destroyed and the thing looked
something like a Jim Vincent spoon. Within two hours of
doing this I took seven pike from swims where previously the
same spoon had spent some ten hours on several days failing
miserably. The same local told me quite firmly that when spinning
and trolling addition of weights and anti-kink vanes to the line
impaired the action of the spoons and was quite detrimental to
success, a story I seem to have read elsewhere in this book.

CHAPTER 15

IRISH PIKING 1971–75

Ray Webb

Five more years have come and gone since I first put pen to paper on Chapter 14 concerning Irish Piking and much of significance has happened in-between times. At that stage (1970) I wrote 'Tried more regularly I am firmly convinced that livebaiting would yield results consistently on a number of waters but it will be left to the visiting English angler to put the matter to the test' and sure enough our holiday-making anglers together with the Dutch, German and French tourists have obtained such encouraging results that snap tackles, bait buckets and brightly coloured bobbins are now firmly established as a regular part of the Irish Piking Scene. To my mind it just had to be so, for before being bought off by the Electricity Supply Board some half a dozen years or so ago, the professional long-liners used to take considerable numbers of pike in addition to the eels they were primarily after, and if their crude conspicuous gear could produce results then the ultra-refined, streamlined tackle of the modern pike men could hardly do otherwise.

As a general rule the livebait enthusiasts have tended to ignore the enormous outsize loughs like Ree and Derg, concentrating their efforts on the smaller fisheries of up to a couple of miles or so in length, waters which can be fully covered by a mobile angler in two or three days' fishing. After a brief but comprehensive scout round with an echo sounder, the resultant depth contour map gives the angler a good idea of the likeliest spots to fish and wherever one happens to be in Ireland there's almost invariably a water somewhere in the area absolutely teeming with perch, one of the best of all livebaits for Irish pike whose natural diet so often consists of very little else. One of my own initial attempts at livebaiting in Ireland proceeded very much along these lines for I elected to fish Lough Scur near Drumshambo, a fishery of about the same overall size as Hornsea Mere—around 400 acres or thereabouts. Caught without an echo sounder my depth map was compiled from an 8 feet inflatable dinghy by means of a rope terminating in a rock heavy enough for one to feel it hitting the bottom. A plentiful supply of live perch was quickly obtained from the Shannon at Ballintra Lock. Accompanied by young Ivor Evans, a pike enthusiast who had caught and seen many fish taken on artificials but never a single one on livebait, I soon put this right by hauling out a lively 7-pounder before he'd had time to fix up tackle and by the end of the day with three more taken up to around the 8 lb mark I could see my young friend was beginning to realize there was more to pike fishing than just trolling a copper and silver spoon. Fishing alone the following day a 14½-pounder saw my hopes of a twenty rising rapidly and at the third attempt, with Ivor and his father in attendance, I struck into a fish that tore away with sufficient speed and power to half convince all three of us that this was the one. From past experience, however, I knew only too well how the tremendous fighting powers of Irish pike could deceive the visiting English angler into thinking he'd hooked into a much bigger fish than was actually the case and sure enough on finally being brought close enough to the surface for an initial glance I could see that it was in fact several pounds short; the length was there but not the girth. Eventually hauled ashore by Ivor it proved to be a long thin fish, superbly conditioned, that tipped the scales at 16½ lb, a most gratifying start to my Irish livebaiting career. Shortly afterwards, from another smaller fishery still in the same area, I hit the jackpot with a fine pike of 24½ lb, my third biggest ever, the successful bait being a lively rudd of around 3 or 4 inches in length. This most encouraging early success and subsequent investigations leave me in no doubt that comparable results and better can be obtained by the enthusiastic livebaiter from the smaller fisheries at many points around the country.

Since those days, however, the livebait enthusiasts have turned their attentions to the bigger loughs too, moving into areas where pike shoals have been located by the local trolling men. Calling in to see Gary Kenny, angling adviser at Portumna, early this year I was informed that a couple of visiting English anglers, fishing Lough Derg near the Bunowen River-mouth, an area long favoured by trolling men, had just taken a number of good pike on livebait

the best of which at 24 lb was the biggest from the area so far
for the year. Though only at Portumna for two or three days on
this particular occasion a couple of Dutchmen resident and working in the town also took pike to 17 lb while I was there, once
again the successful bait being a live perch. Farther up the Shannon, Lough Ree too is also producing pike to livebait, Dave
Cumpstone taking four 20-pounders to 26 lb by this method in
a mere couple of months' fishing, two of which were taken on
the same day. He's also turned up a couple of 29-pounders this
way but it can be slow, laborious work as I found out the hard
way when I teamed up with him in 1974, for after flogging away
at several different areas for a full three weeks of all-out effort we
finished up with virtually nothing to show at the end of it, not
even small jack pike in anything like the numbers. I'd have done
far, far better by trolling a 3-inch brass spoon.

In addition to the stillwater fisheries, large and small, the Irish
rivers are being subjected to more and more livebaiting with each
succeeding year, as a glance at the Specimen Fish List will confirm; obscure, previously unheard-of waters like the Breensford
River near Athlone and the Castle River at Killoshandra cropping
up with pike over the 20 lb mark in the last couple of years. The
larger more famous rivers too are producing really top-class
results, the Shannon at Ballintra Lock near Drumshambo producing specimen pike to livebait year after year, the top man in
this line being Jacques Piraprez, a Belgian who was until recently
living and fishing full time from a barge moored in the river. Completely indifferent to the attractions of artificials Jacques fished
nothing but livebait, anchoring his boat out in the stream,
employing a 16½ feet rod to work his bait under the branches and
amidst the sunken roots of the bushes and trees to be found
growing in profusion along the banks of these upper reaches of
the river. Offering his services as a guide and supplier of livebait,
Jacques' all-round knowledge and expertise was a sound investment for the newcomer to the area with only a week or a fortnight
to spare. The biggest pike to livebait I can find recorded from
this stretch of the river is the 31-pounder taken on April 25th 1972
by Maurice Cullen of Drumshambo, and a really tremendous fish
to be landed from a rocky snag-ridden torrent of roaring, tumbling
highly paced water more commonly associated with the migratory
salmon than the supposedly sluggish slack-water-loving pike.

Branching off the main Shannon at Shannonbridge the Suck is one of the many tributaries that offer first-class sport to the live-bait enthusiast for the annual large run of grilse salmon, the vast bream shoals and the clear fertile limestone nature of the water providing all that is needed to grow really pig pike in considerable numbers. Travelling through Ballygar in 1972 I was called into Patsy Scanlen's tackle shop to view a remarkable brace of pike, both dead unfortunately, as is so often the case in Ireland—though determined efforts are now being made by the Inland Fisheries Trust to educate visiting and local anglers into putting them back alive. Stretched out on the floor while waiting for the official photographer to roll up was a full 50 lb of pike, made up of one fish too many perhaps, but at 24 and 26 lb only the most demanding of specimen hunters would complain. The larger of the two fish was taken by a casual angler spinning a copper and silver spoon but the 24-pounder was hauled out by a visiting angler from France who set up pike tackle terminating in a 1½ lb jack pike for livebait, an offering that was accepted almost immediately on being cast out. Farther downstream on the same river Ned Caulfield of Ballinesloe put a specimen of 29 lb on the Big Fish List taken, as he believed, on a live roach which was no doubt a live rudd, for the Irish angler regularly confuses the two species.

For lovers of canal fishing both the Royal running from Dublin to join the Shannon at Clondra and the Grand from Dublin to Shannon Harbour contain a vast head of pike with numerous double-figure fish and a sprinkling of twenties, far more than is generally realized I'm sure. Indeed, the biggest pike officially recorded in the rivers section of the Specimen Fish List for 1974 came from the Grand Canal and if that isn't a true spot of traditional Irish I'd like to know what is. Fishing the water for a brief three or four days early in 1973 I met several anglers who'd taken double-figure pike there on livebait at various times and the List officially records a 20 lb 2 oz specimen from Ferbane in July 1970 taken on a live perch. In such shallow, gin-clear water I'd be inclined to use a transparent bubble float rather than a cork bung which must inevitably be extremely conspicuous so close to the bait.

With livebaiting so much a part of the scene these days the Inland Fisheries Trust have introduced a scheme to supply bait for anglers who haven't the time or the inclination to obtain their own. At a cost of 5p per fish and ordered at least one full week in advance the Trust undertake to supply livebait at several points around the country, to be collected by the angler between 9 and 11 a.m., Saturdays and Sundays excepted. Roach livebait may only be used in the Erne System, where they are already well established, for every effort is being made to stop the species spreading to other waters. All enquiries for livebait should be addressed to The Development Manager (Bait), Inland Fisheries Trust, Mobhi Boreen, Glasnevin, Dublin, 9.

When bait prove difficult to keep alive in times of hot dry weather the sporting prospects remain good, for the Irish pike tend to take a suspended deadbait just as readily as a live one. Indeed, some anglers hold that the bigger pike around 20 lb and over are more likely to be taken on a suspended deadbait for then they don't have to waste time and energy chasing their meals. True or false, I can vouch personally for the efficiency of deadbait fished a couple of foot or so off the bottom, for out on Doon Lough at Broadford County Clare on a cold wet and windy day late on in April I took 9 pike to 10½ lb in a short afternoon's fishing all on dead rudd and I do mean dead: they were literally stinking to high heaven. Four days later with the arrival of the third anticyclone since the middle of March I was out fishing the same swim once again, accompanied by Colin Campbell and his friend, Eamon, of Newmarket-on-Fergus, finding the fish feeding to suspended dead rudd as before, taking pike of 4 lb, 11 lb and 22 lb, the latter being photographed virtually all the way from the take to the net and on to the final weigh-in and return. Not that these successes came as any great surprise to me, for back in June of 1973 fishing near Carrick on Shannon I'd taken, amongst a number of smaller fish, a fine pike of 22 lb 12 oz all the captures being made on suspended deadbait, the big one coming to a 7 oz bream some 2 or 3 days dead. On Kinale near Finea on the Inny, a large number of big pike have been taken in recent years on suspended dead perch. At numerous other venues around and about the length and breadth of the country regular successes are being constantly recorded, so lack of livebait need deter no one provided a few dead perch, rudd, herrings or sprats are available.

In the trolling sphere too deadbaits mounted on Archer or Ariel tackle are coming into the picture more and more each year; the Piker's Club men fishing on Lough Allen have achieved

tremendous results over the last three or four years trolling dead
perch. Many of Roy Smyth's best fish were taken in this fashion.
He did in fact borrow a couple of dead rudd from me when I
was on Lough Allen myself in 1974 and took pike of 8 and 9 lb
on a scorching hot, dead calm day in the middle of a seven-week
long heatwave when the fish were understandably difficult to
tempt, while in August of the preceding year Paddy Reynolds'
brother Sean hauled out a superb specimen of 31 lb. This one too
fell to a dead perch. Many of Dave Cumpstone's early pike from
Lough Ree came to a dead perch trolled behind a slowly moving
boat, both on the outboard and the oars, including a fine fish of
around the 27 lb mark, but as previously stated he's switched to
livebaiting in recent years convinced that he's in with a better
chance of a 30-pounder that way.

For casting and retrieving, sink and draw style, deadbaits are
perhaps at their very best, fished from either bank or boat,
anchored or moving; such is the considered opinion of Harold
Pattison, the former Rochdale angler now living and working in
Dublin. Top-class matchman, twice winner of the Ulster Open,
placed second in the River Bann in September 1972, inventor of
the Spring Tip and Golden Glo deadbait dye and expert all-round
specimen hunter, Harold plumps solidly for deadbait fished sink
and draw as the best method for catching pike, small, medium and
large on so many of the best known Irish fisheries. Firmly established as way out ahead of all other techniques on the Grand Canal,
one of Harold's favourite pike and match waters, it successfully
lured and landed a 22 lb specimen for him on January 23rd 1972
and a string of big doubles 18, 17, 16, 14-pounders and so on the
following winter, though this time without a twenty. My own
brief shot at the Grand Canal pike produced a brace of 12 and
14 lb to sink and draw deadbait and doubtless I could have taken
many more but I decided to push on to Lough Derg in hopes of a
better chance of bigger fish, a decision that couldn't have been
altogether wrong for I finished up there with pike of 18, 19 and
20 lb 2 oz, the latter winning me the Gary Kenny Trophy for
1973.

Though much initial trial and error experimentation has been
carried out with live and suspended deadbaiting since 1970, enough
to firmly establish both methods as highly successful pike takers,
the position as regards ledgered deadbaiting, my own favourite

technique, remains very much the same as it was, little work
having been carried out in this direction over the intervening
years. Harold Pattison's ledgered deadbaiting carried out over
several winters on a large variety of waters was finally abandoned
in disgust, the returns obtained failing dismally to justify the
effort involved. On the other hand Colin Campbell, operating on
the waters around Tulla and Ennis in County Clare has taken the
odd pike or two to ledgered mackerel tail—fish up to 14 lb or so—
and he knows of one or two others taken on the same technique
in the area. A newcomer to the game of a mere couple of years'
experience, Colin's results are far more encouraging than they
would be if obtained by an accomplished long established pike
man but he's coming along rapidly (as is only to be expected, for
I'm training him myself!) and the next year or two ahead could
well see the outsize County Clare pike succumbing to the ledgered
deadbait with ever-increasing frequency. It's quite on the cards
really for the River Erne has produced a number of big pike to
the method over the last four years and so has Lough Derg on
the River Bann in Northern Ireland where George Higgins has
taken so many of his best fish. If only mackerel and herrings were
more regularly and widely available around Ireland I'd feel far
more optimistic, for I know from years of personal experience
how good these two baits can be. On the brighter side, however,
in most areas small trout are not too hard to come by and though
I've rarely had the opportunity to try them out myself many
anglers who have, Dick Walker included, assure us that they are
absolutely deadly; one of the best deadbaits of all. So viewed all
round weighing up this against that, the efficiency of the ledgered
deadbait technique in Ireland is still very much in the balance. Much
remains to be done before an overall decision can be reached one
way or the other. Enough has already been achieved however to
convince me that in certain areas at any rate a top class experienced
English deadbaiter could well surprise the angling world in
general and the local enthusiasts in particular with the size and
number of pike taken. Be that as it may the use of fish, live or
dead, for pike baits is already proven beyond all doubt as a glance
at the Specimen Fish Lists for the period 1970 to 1974 will amply
show, for of 65 specimen pike recorded well over half the total
(35 in fact) fell to a fish bait of one sort or another. With such
encouraging returns already established the live and deadbait

enthusiasts from England, Holland, Germany and the other European countries, men who are brought up to that sort of thing, can book their holidays in Ireland confident in the knowledge that they can expect the very best of sport by using the tackles and techniques they know best and prefer.

CHAPTER 16

OTHER PIKE ANGLERS ENCOUNTERED

Ray Webb

In these days when specimen-hunting groups spring up like mushrooms here, there, and everywhere, the tendency is for mass attacks on our pike fisheries. Parties of up to nine or more anglers out together for a day is a regular occurrence. Doubtless much can be learned from these combined efforts that would pass undetected by a man fishing alone, though not all pike fisheries by any means can stand such intensive fishing for any length of time. By inclination and temperament a number of anglers who seek out the bigger fish tend only to enjoy their sport if operating alone, or with just one or two companions. Their nature is such that the sight of brolly and baskets stretching out along the bank as far as the eye can see takes all the pleasure out of the day's outing. I myself fall very much into this category, independence of thought and action being virtually essential if life is to have any meaning for me at all. At the same time I'm well aware that mass co-operation in the matter of theory can improve one's chances out of all recognition. Provided we are not all out together on the same water on the same day, the more anglers brought into a discussion on ideas, experiences, tips and tactics the better. Two heads are better than one and all the rest of it. In addition to the benefits derived from the interchange of ideas there is the enjoyment afforded by the meeting up with like-minded men. Pike anglers as a rule are men of determination and character, well worth knowing. They just have to be to stick it out, week in week out right through the worst of the winter weather we experience in this part of the world.

One astonishing fellow, the type of angler to be found nowhere else on earth but in Ireland, I met up with one day sitting on a bridge spanning a tiny stream in County Sligo. Before I'd been in the area long I'd found out that this was his invariable custom every afternoon. One's clock could be set by his appearance at the bridge and I began to look forward eagerly to enjoying a regular chat. Some of the tales he told could be guaranteed to have one fair rocking with laughter; all wrapped up with humour and a touch of blarney as only an Irishman knows how. Rods were scornfully rejected as new-fangled inventions of no account. Monofilament too was similarly classified, the line he favoured being a cuttyhunk type product of shark-fishing proportions, the end of which, on one occasion out in the boat when he was trolling, was securely tied to his knee. As luck would have it this was the day he latched into his biggest-ever pike, a monster of some 33 or 34 lb: successfully boated in the end but the agony that man must have gone through before the successful conclusion was achieved just doesn't bear thinking about. A small lightly built fellow, with a hard-fighting summer pike of thirty pound plus attached via a tight line to his person, it wouldn't have surprised me in the least to have heard of him being hauled over the side of the boat into the lake and towed round at high speed much after the fashion of the water skiers who appear with ever-increasing frequency on our fisheries these days. Improving his technique on later excursions the line was tied not to himself but to the oar, so imparting life and action to the spoon bait as the boat was rowed along. In the event of a take the oar was thrown into the water, being seen bobbing along the surface till the pike was finally exhausted and ready to be brought aboard. A really time-honoured method this, of course, allowing a fish to play itself out against a buoyant object; the natives along the Amazon were catching monstrosities of seven feet in length by this device centuries ago.

On my first trip to Horsey Mere in 1965 I was fortunate enough to meet up with Bill Giles, the Norwich schoolmaster and his regular partner Reg Sandys. This was as good a way to start one's fishing on that particular sheet of water as one could have hoped for. A man with a fine command of the facts and statistics of his many years of experience on the Broads, Bill showered me with enough information in a matter of a few hours' conversation to send me out on to the Mere as confident of success as if I'd been haunting the water week in and week out for a decade or more. Events proved this confidence to be well founded too, for a 24¾-pounder was boated in double quick time beating my previous best by some 2¼ lb. It was Bill in fact who first convinced me of the efficiency of a deadbait suspended off the bottom, especially in times of rough blustery weather. I was also surprised to learn that he mounted his ledgered deadbaits the 'wrong' way round with the treble hooks pointing towards the head instead of away from it in the universally adopted manner. Apparently, so many of Bill's takes occurred as the ledgered deadbait was being retrieved that he'd plumped for this reversed hooking arrangement claiming that the more normal runs that developed with the bait being held hard on the bottom were hooked just as effectively as with the standard tackle set up. One of the most successful pike men of all time with over thirty 20-pound pike to his credit Bill's opinions must be accorded serious consideration, unusual though they may at times appear.

Down on the waters in the Cambridgeshire area I've done quite a lot of fishing over the years with Bill Chillingsworth of Little Paxton, another angler who dedicates all his winters exclusively to the pursuit of pike. Like myself, Bill is a great believer in the efficiency of chub as a livebait. One of the reasons he lives alongside the Great Ouse I'm sure is to ensure a plentiful supply of these tireless workers. A method that Bill employs quite a lot is to float fish a deadbait with the depth set so that the herring just doesn't quite hold the bottom, but rolls round in an arc to the pull of wind or current. Since it is noticeable that Bill is usually well up in the running whenever the herring is taking any fish at all, this most unusual technique is I'm convinced well worth a try on other waters too. If I have learnt a thing or two from Bill from time to time the score was levelled in decisive fashion one day regarding the supernatural effect of my old primus stove. In the Hornsea hot years it was amazing the number of times Johnny Neville and I sat for hours without a run only to see the line snaking off the reel as soon as the chips were in the frying pan and the stove roaring away. Inevitably of course, the stove had to be switched off, a procedure that was often repeated as many as four times in one day before we were finally able to get a meal prepared. Explaining its magical powers to Bill Chillingsworth and his wife Sheila on the banks of the Ouse one day, I could see I was being received with a scepticism they were trying hard to conceal. 'Okay,' says I. 'Now is as good a time as any, we have been at it for five hours without a run. I'll give you a practical demonstration', firing up the primus there and then. Within the minute Bill's float had shot away and he hauled out a lively 5-pounder. He turned round to face me with considerably more respect than he'd shown formerly, but I'd no time for chat since my own bung had just disappeared with an audible 'plop'. Dashing down the bank I heard Sheila call that she'd bring the landing net but Bill wouldn't hear of it—'Never mind the net' he commanded, 'you just stand by and make sure the stove doesn't go out, that's your little job for the moment.' I could see my point had been well and truly proven.

Though my fishing with Fred Wagstaffe and Bob Reynolds has been confined to the summer of 1970 only, in the four weeks we spent together I was as impressed by the all-round knowledge, depth of thought and practical ability of these two remarkable anglers as I've ever been impressed before or since. Sitting up swopping yarns and experiences into the small hours night after night, it soon became obvious to me just how and why they had such a tremendous tally of outsize specimens to their credit. After eating, sleeping and drinking fishing for so many years the big ones just had to come their way. Inseparable angling companions over the years, they have developed a working partnership of incredibly high efficiency. Their boat drill for instance is a model for all young enthusiasts to copy. Seeing them take their thirteen feet boat, Black Pig, out into a really rough water for the first time I was immediately struck by the likeness to a crew of professional fishermen going out with the North Sea Trawler Fleet; all kitted out in oilskins, sou'westers, gumboots and what have you, scuppers awash and water spraying up everywhere. On that particular day not one angler in a hundred would have ventured forth but the old Black Pig struggled valiantly out of the gale-lashed harbour, across the roughest section of the lake, finally winning through to calmer water on the far side. Furthermore a number of good pike were taken, a triumph for teamwork and determination if ever I saw one. No mean scribes these men, either, their week by week column that ran in *Angling Times* throughout the summer of 1970 being one of the most successful and widely read features ever to appear in print. Such was the impact of this serial that when one lady admirer went to her local bookstall and asked for a copy of Fred and Bob every week till November, in spite of the general merriment that ensued, the newsagent knew straightaway which journal she required.

Over in Holland doing a spot of piking in 1962 I was fortunate enough to meet up with Willem Persoons, the Amsterdam tackle dealer, top angler and official keeper of the records for that country. In a land where drainage of the low lying fen type territory has always been a major problem and industrial pollution down to an absolute minimum, he was well situated indeed to knock up an impressive score of big fish, as he had in fact done over the years. It was on this trip that I first realized the suitability of multiplying reels for pike fishing. The Dutch anglers almost invariably use these products in conjunction with rods ringed above rather than below the fibreglass blanks as in this country. A technique employed by Willem on one of the narrow drains we fished was to take out his boat, a heavy metal-hulled job, with a supply of livebait aboard and row slowly along towing a 5 oz roach mounted on the traditional set up, with cork bung attached, some 25 yards or so in our wake. Up to that time I'd never heard of anyone trolling livebait, as you might term the method, but it proved highly successful even on that three foot deep drain, where we might well have expected to scare the living daylights out of all the pike. We rowed virtually right over the top of their heads. Since that time I've come across several other anglers who have employed this technique with outstanding success. Beyond all doubt there are times and places where it is far and away the best bet of all. Unlike this country, where spoons and plugs are rarely used for big pike, the cast and retrieve method is commonly practised in Holland. It achieves notable results as a regular thing. Ilse, Bill's wife, in fact had reached the 25 lb mark with pike on spinner, the photograph of which is one of the first things to catch the eye when entering their shop.

On the shores of Lough Allen one day, I was just beaching the boat when a large black limousine with a touring caravan on tow drew up at the side of the pier. Out stepped an old fellow, intrigued like everyone else by my catamaran-type boat. The talk as always turned to fish and fishing. An old military man, he had done his share of globe-trotting apparently, and he promptly brought out, for my inspection, an array of rods, reels and other items of tackle that still managed to look old fashioned even in comparison with mine. The ferrules on one fly rod, manufactured in Cork around the turn of the century if I remember aright, incorporated a pin that fell into a locking position after a half turn, and even after such a lengthy passage of time the working condition of this device was still first-class, no play being in evidence at all. Still keenly interested in all the latest developments, travelling around and fishing completely alone, he was in fact 74 years young! I rejoiced for the umpteenth time at this latest example of the way our great sport can keep a man active and enthralled all the way along to old age.

In the same area too I spent a lot of time in the company of Mr. P. J. (Paddy) Reynolds of Drumshambo, a pike fisherman extraordinary. Winner in the match-angling sphere of the All Ireland and the Irish National events, bream catcher, eel catcher, salmon man and anything else you care to mention, Paddy's greatest love however was undoubtedly the pike, 20-pounders having fallen to his copper spoons with gay abandon over the years. An hour's chat with Paddy before I first went out to tackle Lough Allen saw me as informed as I ever could be on the theory involved. It only remained for me to get out there and put it into practice. Just how many big pike Paddy has taken I really couldn't say but his biggest went all of 48 lb and that was weighed without the head! As a guest-house owner, and boat owner (his family being known as 'the boat Reynolds' to distinguish them from the many others of the same name in the area), Paddy is an extremely busy man. He is hard to contact at times, but well worth seeking out. It took me five days to catch up with him when I was last in Drumshambo. Those five days of searching were well spent, believe me. His information and advice being as sound as I ever came across.

These then are some of the many worthwhile and interesting characters I have met in my never-ending quest for bigger and better pike. A species that can keep men of this calibre fascinated by its pursuit year after year must surely warrant all the protection we can afford to save it from the extinction so many anglers seem bent upon bringing about.

II

When one is young one is inclined to think the most important thing about fishing is catching big fish. I think it was Richard Walker who once told me that, for him, the company he keeps is more important still. No one could accuse R. W. of requiring excuses for failing to catch big fish, and I am inclined to set great store by his remark. The reader, I hope, will not accuse Ray and myself of failing to catch big fish, and we also get inestimable enjoyment from the company of one or two fellow pikers. I *prefer* fishing on my own, and I am sure other anglers on the bank feel the same way about my presence, but I would go on record as saying that the thousands of hours spent in the company of other members of the Cambridgeshire Pike Anglers have made those blank days most agreeable. 'Loners' are always amongst the most interesting of pike anglers—the sort of person you find trolling the wilderness of an Irish lough—particularly if you can get them to impart information. Dave Cumpstone of Derby is of this ilk, and although not applauded in the angling press (his choice) he is without question one of the most successful anglers of our time. He is a loner, and no mistake, using his boat for transport along the Shannon system, sleeping on islands or in the boat. And really getting to know the water and the fish. He was extremely generous to Christine and I, in our more mundane efforts on the Irish waters, providing angling information and loan of equipment quite readily. Regrettably we have 'lost' him, and, as in the way with loners, have now no idea of the where-abouts of his latest angling exploits. One gets whispers of similar characters when pursuing the angling literature: shadowy people who catch immense fish and yet shun publicity. Their contribution to the future of angling is very much at the personal level, and it is common to find them most warm and generous.

There are other pikers, more retrievable socially, who are nevertheless quite difficult to find on a day at the waterside. Roy Hatherley of Edgware, who has given us so much information about ledgered herring fishing, is one: to find his car parked down a fenland lane is no guarantee that you will find Roy. He will be well away from roads quietly searching the water with herrings and mackerel which he fishes in every manner from quite static to relatively mobile. Dug Taylor of York, who gets more runs on deadbait than any pike fisherman that I know, is similar only worse: Dug used to take me fishing in an old three-wheeler, fibreglass, Reliant van and would then disappear into the distance to reappear at dark having had more runs in one day than I could achieve in a season, or so it seemed! Both Roy and Dug are keen on deadbaiting for pike and it must be admitted that this aspect of piking has great attraction for those who like to carry a couple of light, ten feet rods, a small rucksack, and a few herrings and mackerels. They can wander off, search the water, relax, and get lost in the countryside as easily as any game fisherman wielding his fly rod and hip flasks.

I have also met a number of lone pikers addicted to less conservative techniques, who like to get away from it all in order to practise those techniques out of sight of prying eyes. Ray and I once found a chap, miles from anywhere on an East Yorkshire drain, who appeared to be fishing quite traditionally with bung tackle, trotting it slowly down the gentle stream. He did not note our approach, and it was only when he swung in his tackle to recast that we realized that his bait was a horizontal sausage mounted on a snap tackle. Yes, he did catch pike occasionally, he said, and that was all we could get him to say. Have we missed out on a new technique here do you think? I simply dare not, in the company of Laurie Manns and Hugh Reynolds, mount up a horizontal sausage—or a vertical one for that matter.

And then there were the bacon boys. No, not chub fishermen, but pike anglers using match rods and sea rods, paternoster tackle and bacon strips. Each bacon strip was some three inches by four, uncooked, and, it was claimed, dangled attractively in the current. These blokes were well away from the main road and yet, come lunchtime they decided to retire to the pub for an hour. Two of them reeled in their tackle but the third asked me if I would watch his rod whilst he was downing a pint! Still too shattered to speak, I nodded my head, and sat there for the next hour, during which time not the faintest sign of a run occurred. I will admit that I spent more time watching his rod than mine. Eventually the bacon boys were seen tottering back along the bank and as they reached me they pounced, with one accord, upon the rod they had left behind, the slender tip of which had just started to tap tap. Pandemonium followed as a sizeable pike tore up and down the weed beds. It transpired that the line was around 6 lb b.s. and the hook tied to a nylon trace. After some hair-raising runs the pike was gradually drawn to the net, and as it slid to the rim the line parted quietly and the fish turned smoothly out into the deeps. So I nearly saw a good pike, approximately 17 lb, landed on dangling bacon. If you think this an unlikely tale I would add that Bob Benton of the Cambridge Specimen Club landed six pike in succession on bacon strip that he was using to catch chub on the middle reaches of the Great Ouse. Bacon may have some future as a pike bait. Sausages, well I ask you. . . .?

Amongst these more reprehensible types I would include the Barmy Lads of Hull (or thereabouts). Ray and I found this sheepish bunch of twelve-year-olds skulking far from the access points of a well known Hull drain. Again we noticed their reluctance to lift their apparent bung outfits from the water, and when they did oblige the reason was starkly apparent. Below each bung hung a veritable barbed wire system of snaptackles with no less than six livebaits to each tackle. The baits were supposed to be more or less one above the other, but the degree of tangling was impressive. They deflated us within seconds by telling us of a 17 lb fish that they had taken the day before from the same spot. I've heard of simulating a shoal of fish before, but this was aggressive fishing to say the least. And anyway six livebaits have to last *me* six weeks sometimes.

And so it goes on. Whilst carp and tench fishermen can be found universally ledgering potatoes or lobworms, the pike-fishing brigade seems to have a high proportion of blood-curdling types. It would be uncharitable of me to paint a picture of one Webb himself at this juncture, yet several friends reading the manuscript for us have threatened to expose both of us as more or less insane. As Ray says, the sport apparently keeps one young; which is presumably why he retired at forty!

CHAPTER 17

PRE-SEASON PREPARATION

Barrie Rickards

Pike fishing begins each year either on June 16th along with all other coarse angling, or on October 1st in River Authority areas where the pike has protection during the summer. It is not my aim to discuss the pros and cons of summer protection for pike, but to get on immediately with pre-season preparation which differs somewhat in the two cases.

Few pike anglers will have livebait-snatching problems in the summer, so that little thought need be put into catching and storing bait. From March to June the usual procedure for all coarse anglers is to overhaul rods, reels, lines, floats, hooks, and other equipment, and for the pike angler it need be no different. All these things can be done enjoyably and the angler be fully ready by June 16th. Since artificials can be so deadly in the warmer months a good deal of inventive effort can go into making plugs and spoons, and in particular those types not yet available on the commercial market. There may be problems with fresh deadbaits such as herrings and mackerel: they are not always available in the summer just when you need them. The answer to this one is to put a small stock in the freezer of your refrigerator, or into a deep freeze if your wife has reached that stage of keeping up with the Joneses of the seventies or, possibly, persuade your supplier or butcher to put them in *his* deep-freeze. Deadbaits such as roach, rudd and gudgeon can also be preserved in formalin prior to the season opening: this is merely a question of getting a small bottle of the stuff from the chemist and asking him how to prepare it for use and avoid getting poisoned at the same time. Jim Gibbinson, our Essex contact, has had considerable success with wobbled, formalin-preserved roach, and clearly the smell of formalin on the bait does not put pike off as many pundits have claimed. The smell of formalin might very well put off the fishermen, but that is a somewhat different matter.

With care then the pike angler can be ready on June 16th with a completely renovated set of tackle, and all his baits except livebaits, which are no problem, and freshly-killed deadbaits, which are the *same* problem. Quite what we shall do if, and when, the ordinary coarse fish Close Season is abolished I do not know. Certainly some aspects of the *intensity* of fishing will change, and I suspect that tackle will not get the same care and attention. Some of the following remarks about preparation for the autumn start also apply to the summer start, and many of the ideas presented in the chapter as a whole are applicable to angling during the season itself. There are many things that one thinks about all the time during the actual fishing, the supply of livebait being just one.

It is assumed here that the piker's rods, artificials, miscellaneous tackle and formalin-preserved deadbaits will be all fully up to scratch on October 1st. Herring and mackerel deadbaits become more easily accessible, at least in my own area, and yet I usually keep a dozen or so in the freezer just in case. Livebaits, however, become extremely difficult to obtain as the cold weather approaches or at least they are difficult to obtain with the regularity that you need them. The answer is to stockpile them prior to October 1st. There is no need to go mad, of course; just a few tens of well chosen sizeable baits are all that are required for a good start. It is worth checking perhaps just to make sure that you are allowed to do this in your own area. Usually you are, unless you go transporting them all over the region. The idea is to live close by your own pike water.

Livebait boxes have been used on the Norfolk Broads for many years by local anglers. A large box of, say, 2 ft × 2 ft × 1½ ft will comfortably hold fifty six-ounce rudd for weeks if necessary, and at the same time keep them fit and healthy. They can be fed, of course, but also obtain a great deal of food in the way of water shrimps which live in the cracks of the box. Indeed, whatever they eat they actually seem to become very healthy in captivity, and provide far better baits than fish caught and carried and used on the same day. My own boxes are built to approximately the above dimensions in half- or three-quarter inch soft wood, with good solid hinges and a padlock. The last item is of quite minor importance since where I keep my own boxes they are unlikely to be tampered with, but I can imagine that on some larger club waters it is better to have some protection against the occasional lout. The sheer weight of a bait box would put off most tampering types. Even without rust-proof hinges a bait box will last several seasons. During the usual close-season period they can be removed from the water, scrubbed clean of algae and dried.

Ideally the best place for a bait box is over a clean gravel bottom, well away from any putrid mud or thick rotting weed. In waters with a bit of current they can be placed on the bottom and moored with a rope, and in ponds are probably better kept floating and similarly moored with a rope. Further aeration of the boxes is quite important, and this can easily be achieved by using a brace and half-inch bit to drill numerous holes in the four sides. If the bait box can be so placed that it is over a clean bottom, and yet is overhung by a tree, you have the best of both worlds since the tree prevents any rapid changes of temperature caused by autumn sunshine and cold frosty nights. This is particularly important with boxes kept in ponds. Careful choosing of the site for a box prevents the nuisance of doing it by trial and error. In order to remove bait before fishing it is useful to construct a platform some six inches below water level on to which the box can be slid before opening.

It is not always necessary to stock up a box by catching your bait on tiddler-snatching tackle. Traps can also be used. The best way of all is to trap unwanted rudd or other fish from a carp fishery, thereby doing two jobs at once. One never manages to remove all the unwanted small fish, and one can at least hope that removal of some will result in an improved growth. The traps I have used in the past are quite simple wire or plastic mesh affairs, some three feet long, round in cross section, and with a trap door at one end, and a narrowing cone entrance at the other. The diameter is about eighteen inches. The main problem even with good traps is that they do not necessarily catch fish. Ray once built one out of shiny, new chicken wire, and another out of dark coloured subdued keepnetting. The most likely to succeed, one would have thought, was the latter and yet it remained a clear second best. On some waters and some swims traps are quite useless: it becomes important to really search around. Moving the trap a few feet can often make a difference.

Very large wire keeps, say, 3 ft × 3 ft × 3 ft can be used instead of boxes, and suffer less from aeration problems. The main problem is the wire itself which can be quite damaging to fish. One should either use plastic wire or make a top for the keep and keep it constantly covered with a sack or grass sods. I use grass sods which also have the desired effect of avoiding extreme temperature changes. During the Christmas freeze-up of 1970 my water had an inch of ice everywhere except in the keep where the insulation of the sods kept it quite clear, thereby helping aeration as well as providing a semi-dark environment where the fish lay quietly. Wire-mesh keeps also allow much more fish food into the container, but I also feed them by placing quantities of maggots on the sods through which they slowly wriggle.

A number of pike anglers I know have garden ponds, the sole purpose of which seems to be to support a good head of livebaits. Polythene ponds can be made in any size or shape and if insulated from below with old sacks and newspapers are reasonably resistant to cold snaps. Pond heaters are highly successful in keeping a portion of the water surface always free of ice. I am also acquainted with at least two anglers who have sunk old boats into their garden and either filled them with water or else lined them with polythene sheet first. Of course, if one happens to be house-proud, some sort of effort can be made to make the pond attractive and an asset to the garden. In this context 'garden' may be taken as synonymous with 'worm lawn'.

There is nothing to stop one keeping bait boxes in the garden pond, and many do so. If the pond is polythene it is advisable to have a polythene container. These latter can either be larger-perforated linen baskets, obtainable at most large stores or hardware shops, or distilled water containers which are about 2 ft × 1 ft. Distilled water holders can have holes easily drilled in the side and can be made to stand upright on the bottom of the pond: a lid is made in the top by cutting along three sides of an imaginary square with a pair of scissors. If you do not see what I mean, try Plate 4.2. One colleague uses a wooden bait box in a concrete pond, and paints the inside of the box so that fish can be slid out quite without harm. The polythene containers mentioned will hold about twenty 4 oz fish during the cold winter months, and perhaps ten 4 oz fish when the weather is warmer.

Finally, horse troughs. I recently came up with a superb system of keeping a good healthy stock of livebait. Beg, borrow or

actually buy a standard, farmer's galvanized horse trough. Four
feet long by eighteen inches wide is quite adequate. This I place
at the very back of the garage, on the floor, fill to within one
inch of the top with water, and insulate the sides with polystyrene or sacking if the garage is particularly cold. During cold
weather such a tank will sustain about twenty sizeable baits,
and these can be fed with bread, groundbait, or pellets if the
angler seems to think they need food. For some reason many
anglers think fish will not feed readily in captivity of this kind,
but the rudd I used to keep would consume slices of floating
bread in no time at all. It is quite possible to aerate a horse
trough by means of one of the small aquarium aerators, such as
the Minor or Major. I plug mine in to the light socket and leave it
going constantly. This increases to around thirty the number of
sizeable bait that the tank will sustain, whilst the aerator itself
consumes very little electricity. As far as I know electrical costs
are about the same as leaving on an electric light all the time. A
friend left a Minor pump running for five years non-stop, so you
can get good value out of them.

The great advantage of a horse trough in the garage is that I
merely back up the van the night before fishing and it becomes
only a minute's job to load up the bait the next morning: far
better than catching it, or even collecting it from a bait box in the
pike lake itself. However, I would not advocate that the angler
kept only one string to his bow. Far better to have several of the
above systems in operation, with only a few fish in the care of
each.

At this point we can assume that the would-be piker has his
tackle in good order and his bait supply assured. All he has to do
now is wait for the season to start, and then go pike fishing, *not*
bait snatching. Or is it? Is there nothing else to do during the
close season? It would help to have some plan as to *where* to fish.
Pike location, a specialist subject in itself, is treated in Chapter 11,
but one of the close-season jobs is to look at possible waters and
attempt to assess their potential. Hours spent pottering about
possible pike waters are never wasted, and it is most enjoyable to
construct maps of the water like that depicted in Fig. 3. I also
constructed a card index of what seemed to me to be big pike
waters, although this index is kept up to date during the fishing
season itself by carefully watching newspaper reports on both

a national and local level. My memory being what it is, I prefer to write things down: other may prefer the mental approach. But my own system, anyway, is to have a 3 in×5 in index card on which I enter the details of the fish, and the water, and also my source of information (e.g. *Angling Times* no. 900 or *Angler's Mail* vol. 3 no. 7). I can then go back to the original report and get the full story, and pictures, neither of which can be squeezed on to a three by five index card.

In short, one really keeps one's eyes and ears open, sifting information, recording it in writing where desirable, pottering about from one water to another, making charts and so on. During the spring close season it may be possible, on one's pottering about the lake, to find the pike spawning. This can provide invaluable information if *big* pike are seen spawning, but the water should not be written off if only small fish are seen. Yet other waters rarely seem to have spawning pike, and in any event the angler has to be at the waterside regularly for the spawning period may last only a few days.

Earlier in this chapter I mentioned vans. Expanding the theme a little, it seems to me that just as top people read *The Times*, top pike anglers drive vans! And often virtually live in them. A van is ideal for the serious pike angler. In addition to the usual tackle—in my case I carry the rods 'made up'—we pile in lilos, sleeping bags, chairs, cooking equipment, bait tins, bait boxes, fish traps and the baby's pram. I even have room for a transporting trolley that I am about to construct, and the rest of my fishing tackle. Occasionally I slide in Laurie Manns and *his* tackle on top of this heap and away we go into the night to arrive at the destination just before dawn. Actually, things are not really chaotic, although the very roominess of a van encourages the pike angler to take everything but the sink at least as far as the parking spot. At the rear of my van, near the off-side door, I have a large livebait can, complete with anti-splash device, standing in a polythene bowl. To one side of this, quite out the way, and tied up over the spare wheel, is the rod holdall containing several rods already made up in the manner described in Chapter 7. By the end of November I have a spade tied up in the same place, just in case I have to dig the van out of mud or a snowdrift. Nearer the driving seat than the bait tin is my rucksack, fully packed the night before unless I have a flask of coffee to add. Then, between the rucksack and passenger seat is a large cardboard box, which sits on various useful items such as folding chairs and large polythene bags (for wet nets), and which contains a full change of clothing, particularly socks, sweaters, and wellington boots. The same box also contains emergency food supplies, including soft drinks, and spare bits of fishing tackle such as reels and pike line.

Behind the driver's seat is a livebait snatching rod and canvas bag with hooks, baits, groundbait, disgorgers and the like. The rod is made up, but broken down into three pieces. It takes me one minute exactly to start tiddler snatching if the occasion arises. There is a spare umbrella here too, partly because two are often better than one in really foul weather, and partly to weigh down the made-up livebait rod to stop it tangling up.

Obviously there is a great deal more space in the vehicle, and it is into this that Laurie and his tackle fits. Before the nipper reached two years old, we had a pram in this space so Laurie used to hang off the roof! Bait boxes, traps and keeps can also be fitted in when required, and we always have a box with paraffin stoves, cookers and a spare can of petrol. This ready-for-anything approach cannot be adopted with the average family car. Finally, in addition to all that I can fit in lilos, sleeping bags, and tent and associated equipment. Thinking about this sort of planning is best done during the close season, mock-up arrangements can be tried, as well as suitable containers for this and that. The entire aim should be to provide as much time as possible, on the day, for pike fishing itself.

As a matter of fact, underlying this apparently careful planning there is an opportunist at work! I believe in planning to such an extent that I can take advantage of rare opportunities which arise, and apply this to other fishing than pike. A few anglers, Fred Wagstaffe amongst them, believe in fishing for one species, in our case pike, for month in and month out year in and year out until they really *understand* the species.

Most of us lesser mortals cannot resist the opportunist approach. Quite recently Christine and I were trolling on Lough Ree and had had one double-figure fish, when Christine hooked a large bream on a 7 in wobbling spoon. After a few moments it shed the hook, but by then we had spotted large bream rolling in the waves. It just *happened* that I had a tin of red worms, a couple of reels with 5 and 6 lb line and two spare rods! The result of half an hour's interlude was bream of 6 lb 1 oz, 7 lb (two) and 7¼ lbs. No doubt some will say this is no way to fish for pike, and they would be right: we certainly enjoyed getting those bream, but it is debatable whether we could claim any credit. In fact we were so overjoyed that I bashed the van on the way home, for the first, and I hope the last time.

Supposing we have done all this preparation, what is it like on the day? What is the plan here? I shall describe my journey to the water on October 1st at the start of a new season: it really applies to the start of any new day, and it helps us give a few more valuable (I hope) tips about the overall approach to piking.

Let me say immediately that although I arrive at the water before dawn, I hate getting up in the morning. Bill Giles tells me that he lingers at home for an hour over a large breakfast before setting out, and as he also begins fishing very early all I can say is that he must enjoy getting up. I do not. I am never in the house for more than fifteen minutes before staggering into the van and away. I wake up on the journey. Some people actually get washed before going fishing at this time. I ask you? Anyway the dirt helps to keep the cold out.

I totter downstairs, switch on the kettle for a pot of tea, and then recoup my clothes from where they have been hanging over the central heating vents. The only food I can stand is a dish of grapefruit which helps to wake me up a little. I put on plenty of warm clothing, including a Barber jacket which I consider second to none, for winter fishing anyway. Some people drive to their fishing in shoes and sweaters and then change into boots and jackets at the venue, the idea being that they do not get cold after the warmth of the car. I never could understand this approach to torture. I drive to my fishing in waders that have become quite hot overnight, and wear my jacket in order to build up a real fug between it and my skin. In the glove compartment there are two balaclavas which I leave off until arrival—my only concession to convention. This theory about donning jackets on arrival reminds me of a similar fallacy that spinning keeps the angler warm in winter. Even the mountaineering boys are beginning to realize that keeping on the move can be fatal in extreme conditions. One point about waders and Barber jackets is that the jacket overlaps the boots giving a comfortable and yet quite waterproof all-over protection, so that really dirty dawns can be treated with disdain.

Do not wear string vests if you are inclined to be on the heavy side. One of our club members who shall remain nameless, complained of pains on his chest during a day's piking in the fens. By sitting astride him and forcing him to strip to the waist we found his nipples peeping through the vest, the string of which had cut deeply into his flesh. His brother had to patch him up with strips of Elastoplast!

In summary then I get up fifteen minutes before 'off', get dressed, have a cup of tea, and get out. Into the garage, a quick swish with a net gets the bait for the day, pop it into the back of the van and then away. Actually, as a concession to the family and the neighbours I *push* the van out of the garage, shut the doors quietly, have a last quick check round and . . . oh! yes, the herrings. The last thing I see before leaving is a big notice with the word HERRINGS in bold capitals. Back to the fridge for the deadbait. I always forget those. And that is it, the maximum time allotted to both bed and piking.

The close season is also the time when the pike angler should consider his job.

The serious pike angler needs to have a definite attitude towards his work—that necessity of life which cuts down your fishing to three days each week. I have yet to find a serious pike man who does not get in the 'third day' as often as possible. Even schoolteachers. Have you noticed how many pike men work at the Post Office? No wonder they have had to put up the price of the stamps. And R.A.F. men too: I'll bet they have aerial photos of every pike water in the country.

An awful lot can go wrong in pike fishing. Probably more bites are missed, and more fish dropped off the hooks than in any other sphere of angling. It is essential, therefore, to have every thing as 'right' as you can—plenty of time at the waterside, knowledge of the bait spots on each pike water you fish, a willingness to fish from dawn till dusk, and willingness and ability to move to new swims with a load of tackle. It all begins at home in the fishing room or shed—the planning that is. If you have in your van, or on the roof of the van, tackle and equipment to suit every contingency then you are well on the way. And of course you will be keeping a file, mental if not on paper, of the regions from which big pike are being caught. I think it can be summed up by saying that you need the willingness

and ability to go any place at any time with the right tackle and
gear: or the nearest approach to this ideal that you, in your own
circumstances, can make. The only things it is difficult to guarantee are livebaits, freshly killed deadbaits, and pike. My gear will be
complete, I think, when I have a small boat on the roof, as has
Ray. He has two which join together to make a fifteen-footer for
the big waters. You see what I mean.

II

There is no doubt at all about the vehicle required by a serious
angler, the van has it over the saloon all the way along the line. If
economy is no consideration a Caravette or Dormobile is absolutely ideal since they are virtually purpose-built, but a close
facsimile can be made by the man who buys a van and converts it
to his requirements. With a bit of wit and ingenuity it is surprising
how small a vehicle can be made to meet one's needs. My own,
for example, is a mere five hundredweight model with an 875 cc
engine yet I managed to live comfortably in it for six months
last year, fully equipped for fishing, camping, boating—the lot.
Having lived in this fashion for so many years now I have reached
the stage where I am completely organized though this may not
be immediately apparent to the casual observer. The independence it gives means that a man can literally live right at the
waterside for long periods and is able to get an intimate knowledge
of the fishes' way of life. One point I would insist on is that the
van incorporates a rear engine. With this item aboard, a quick
drive round before settling down for the night will ensure
enough heat rising from the engine to thaw out any chill that
may have crept into the angler's bones during a long winter's day
on the waterside; it really is better than an electric blanket.

My own close season observations of spawning pike have
provided me with information and enjoyment of the highest
order. In my experience it would seem that the pike is largely a
monogamous creature. This is something of a rarity in fish life
generally for tench, roach, chub and the rest shoal up in numbers
ranging anything from five to fifty or more but the pike that I
have been fortunate to observe have always been in pairs. Invariably it is a case of the female being the bigger of the two,

the 20-pounders we all set our sights on seemingly always of the gentler sex. One thing they do have in common with the other species at spawning time is their indifference to human observation. I have approached to within a matter of feet of double-figure pike at this time of year without any difficulty whereas a similar attempt in October could be counted on merely to provide a bow wave. Spawning time apart it is only the jack to 3 lbs or so that I can sneak up close to as a rule, the bigger fish usually prove extremely cagy; for a really good look at them I find a rod and line has to be taken along as well!

As an ex-telephonist I can thoroughly recommend Post Office employment for the dedicated angler, which was the reason for my being there of course. Since it is all evening and night work some part of almost every day can be spent on the bankside provided that the waters are not too far from home. This regular opportunity for angling and observation gives the G.P.O. man a real head start over the two or three days a week angler. Equally important perhaps, in the way of suitable employment for the angler, is the ability to work weekends and to take one's days off in midweek to avoid the ever-increasing pressure on our over-crowded fisheries. From the point where I took up G.P.O. work in 1963, my catches leapt ahead to a most gratifying degree; prior to that I had usually been just missing the desired results but the jackpot has been well and truly hit with some regularity ever since. The ability to study the results obtained by other anglers out over the weekend, to find out the methods employed, which swims were fished, the bait, and so on, and then to get out on the water and to have it to oneself I am sure has been one of the major factors in the tremendous progress achieved.

CHAPTER 18

CONCLUDING REMARKS

Such then are some of the ideas, theories and conclusions arrived at after many years of all-out effort in search of bigger and better pike. If we have failed to land a 30-pounder there is some consolation in the fact that we have made the twenties and double-figure fish sit up and take notice in no uncertain fashion. As it is, the magical 30 lb mark remains to be attained, an incentive to maintain our endless campaign: not that any encouragement would appear to be needed, our enthusiasm remains as keen as ever it was. One season we may do a spot of carp fishing, another it will be the roach that occupies our attention, then a spell after chub or barbel maybe. A variety of species holds a fascination for us over a period of a few months or so but as regards old *Esox* the position over a full fifteen years has never looked like changing. Every season is a pike season as far as we are concerned.

More and more anglers are obviously thinking along the same lines these days, the number of serious pike men increasing with every passing year. In our early days it was a case of Dennis Pye doing his stuff on Hickling Broad and the adjoining waters, and that was about all. As far as the rest of the country was concerned what bit of piking being done took place on a second rod set up while the angler concentrated on his main tackle intended for roach or bream. How different is the position today when every week throughout the winter months at all points around the country dedicated pike men fish exclusively for their favourite species, only putting together the 12½ feet Faststrike when a further supply of livebait is needed. Individually and in groups anglers are studying the ways and capture of the pike as never before and the successes obtained in such a wide diversity of areas affords ample proof of the value of their extremely serious approach. In Leicestershire it is Clive Loveland on Knipton Reservoir: on the drains around Boston. Geof. Bates and company are

taking vast quantities of pike on sink and draw deadbait; down in
Essex Jim Gibbinson's name can be expected to crop up on the
big fish list at any time, and fishing the same area the Wessex
group are going extremely strong when they are not caning
them out on the London Reservoirs that is. On the Norfolk
Broads Pye is no longer going it alone by any means. Frank
Wright, Bill Giles, Reg Sandys and a number of others are all
putting their time in after pike. As a result of such intensive
angling the pike, always in the nature of things far fewer in
numbers than the other species, as can be expected in the case
of an out and out predator, is in dire need of conservation and
careful handling. It is essential as never before that fish are
returned to the water as a matter of course or our sporting
prospects will rapidly decline. The men listed above and many
others of similar calibre are no problem, but the newcomers to
the game and the occasional 'piker' continue to cause concern.
Much of the damage would appear to be done by men who are
actually afraid of the pike they have just caught, having to clout
it on the head before they dare go near enough to set about retrieving the hooks. Education and instruction is the answer.
The responsibility rests with all experienced and informed pike
anglers. It is essential that these offenders are taught just how to
unhook a pike without causing damage if the all too common
sight of dead fish littered about all over the place is to disappear
from the bankside, as indeed it must.

Another great problem concerning all pike enthusiasts is one
of an extremely serious nature indeed, so much so that it warrants
positive action urgently. At a meeting of pike lovers recently all
was going well, a most cordial atmosphere prevailing with all
the signs pointing to a get-together that would prove not only
entertaining but productive as well, when the scientist present,
Dr. Charles Franklin of Chelsea College, took to his feet and
informed us in a calm collected manner that was none the less
effective for all that, of a very real danger, which would, unless a
present trend was checked, see the extermination of the pike
from our fisheries in approximately fifteen years' time. At this, of
course, a chill descended immediately on the gathering, most of
the point of the whole affair being cancelled out. An answer
just had to be found and quickly at that. As Dr. Franklin went on
to explain, the tremendous increase in the use of chemical sprays

of organo-chloride compounds, polychlorinated biphenyls and the likes in agriculture, much of which eventually finds its way into our rivers, can produce blindness, sterility and various other ill effects in the pike, much as has been known to be happening for some time with sea birds along our coasts whose eggs these days steadfastly refuse to hatch out. Not only that, but this one additive, organo-chlorides, is one of the few that is not being taken out of our drinking water as it leaves the reservoirs. As a result of this not only is the pike's future threatened but we also, the population of this country, are, in the long term, being slowly poisoned as well. As previously stated gloom descended like a cloud—and from that point on water was left severely alone: we all drank beer instead! What steps if any are being taken to avoid this complete and final disaster we are still trying to ascertain; the position being so grave that unless something is done our sport and our livelihood too, with those of us professionally engaged in the angling trade, will be in jeopardy. Both pike and humans are predators, both at the head of their respective food chains; and the pike, being a more primitive vertebrate can be expected to succumb to the poisoning first.

For the moment, however, the position is extremely good, great advances in tackle, knowledge and the number of serious pike anglers around resulting in catches generally being far better than ever they were. Glancing through the angling press week after week throughout the winter months twenty-pound pike are cropping up here, there and everywhere, while four 30-pounders were reported from the country as a whole in November alone during 1970. Such incredible catches inevitably result in one hearing with increasing regularity the theory put forward that a twenty-pound pike is no longer a big pike, but on checking up it is invariably found that the speaker does not fish for them himself, being a confirmed roach or bream man or even a non-angler. It is the tremendous upsurge in all-out pike fishing activity that is being completely overlooked of course. The men who actually catch the big ones are under no illusions about 20-pounders, make no mistake about it. These are extremely big fish in England, Ireland, or anywhere else for that matter. It is not just the inexperienced angler, pikewise that is, who tends to hold inflated views on this point. One comes up against it too in men who are holding down top jobs with the angling press, people who are responsible to a large degree for the moulding of public opinion. In September 1969 for instance Fred Wagstaffe rang one journal to break the news of his and Bob Reynold's returns over seven days' fishing on Templehouse Lough in County Sligo. Incredible though it may sound to any well-informed angler the reply he received went something along these lines: 'Five over twenty-five pounds in one week did you say Fred? Yes I thought I had got it correct, that is about right for Ireland'. One thing we can state without fear of contradiction, the chap who gave that as his considered opinion had never caught big pike in Ireland. About right for Ireland indeed. What a comment on what must surely be one of the greatest achievements in pike-fishing history. Another case that can be instanced is the returns recorded on Lough Ree for the first three months' fishing of 1970 during which time the Athlone Anglers Association weekly pike match, with men of intimate knowledge gained from many years' study of the water competing, failed to record one single 20-pounder between them. It is not our intention to run down Lough Ree, far from it. It is in fact one of the greatest of all pike fisheries. What we are trying to do is to show this matter of big pike in its true light, so avoiding disappointment and disillusion that is otherwise inevitably awaiting the newcomers to the sport.

What then, in our opinion is good pike fishing? After really intensive efforts put in on many of the top waters around over a long period we are convinced that a man who is regularly taking fish in the seven-to-twelve pound range has every reason to feel fairly pleased with himself. A double-figure pike a day with perhaps one or two more on odd occasions has always proved to be a reasonable objective in our experience. There is a lot of satisfaction to be had from this achievement. It is our sincere hope in fact that the day never dawns when we are unable to enjoy fishing of this calibre. If it were so then the time would have come to pack up piking once and for all. Over and above this steady build-up of double-figure fish there should always be, as far as we are concerned, some sort of chance of a 20-pounder. Fishing two or three days a week throughout the winter, a couple of pike of this weight or above should be within the realms of probability. If things go really well and the season turns out to be a particularly good one four or five or possibly more, might well be recorded but this sort of return is to be expected as the exception rather than the rule. As fanatical anglers who fish all the year round for most of the commonly found species, coarse and game, we are left in no doubt at all that if we had to restrict our angling to the pursuit of just one alone, then that one would undoubtedly be the pike. Throughout every season, in hot weather or cold, in shallow weedy water or down in the deeps, for top class exciting sport to a variety of methods, livebait, deadbait, spinner, jigging, the lot, the pike really is in a class of its own. A man who devotes himself to the study and capture of this most glorious of all our fishes will experience a fascination and satisfaction that will last him throughout the whole of his life.

SUMMARY

Except when pike are feeding wildly, an unfortunately rare situation, feeding is confined to short periods, but at more regular intervals than is commonly supposed: more or less every day in fact. A 'same time each day' pattern is almost always revealed, each pattern changing dramatically after three to six weeks. Refined techniques are more successful during the 'off' period than chuck it and chance it methods. Ledgered deadbaits are best fished without multihook rigs, and in hotspots and lairs particularly those on shallow or long-established waters, an addition to the tackle such as lead and floats are likely to be detrimental to success *in the long term*; mackerels are better than herrings. Free-line livebaiting is the most successful method of all livebaiting techniques; ledgered livebaiting runs it a close second except when long range or holding in a current is needed, when it tends to be better than free-lining.

Away from hotspots, where mostly hunting pike are encountered, the above methods succeed as well as any others and better than most. On the occasions when a float is needed, the sliding float system described in Chapter 5 is an excellent system which can be quickly converted to paternostering, ledgered deadbait or suspended deadbait.

Artificials will succeed in hotspots, particularly during the warmer months as instanced by the success in the Fenland drains and Irish loughs. Obviously they will pick up hunting pike,

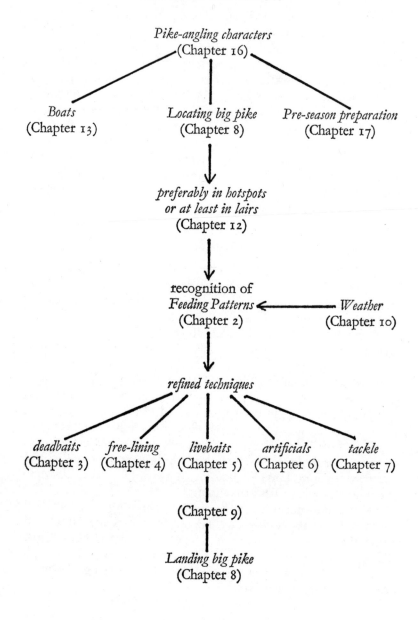

possibly more efficiently than any other method. The expressions one often hears that such and such a water is a 'spinner water' or a 'herring water' are misnomers in that waters change, often rapidly, and pike tend to go off all baits eventually, except livebaits and well-presented artificials of the plug type, or slowly retrieved deadbaits. A good example seen in the history of one of the new still waters. A few years ago, when intensive efforts to get to grips with the pike were first allowed numbers could be caught on spinners of almost any kind. Then followed a period of two or three seasons when wobbling spoons were more effective, taking fish over twenty pounds. Eventually a 'herring' period was reached and spinning of any type became virtually useless. During all this time livebait succeeded well, and is still the most effective method; herring fishing is again good during barometric pressure 'lows' and spinning is pitifully slow. It is interesting, however, that plugs have always, and still do, get reasonable if not spectacular results. Suspended deadbaits run livebaits a close second and have accounted for some good fish.

The careful landing and handling of big pike will become more critical to pike angling as time goes on, since the best way to ruin a big pike water is to remove big pike. All the anti-pike brigade know this. There are good grounds for concern on this matter: the Inland Fisheries Trust of Eire have been removing pike from trout fisheries, probably quite rightly, and the result has been many more smaller pike in the waters and very few big ones. The Inland Fisheries Trust's results would stand any statistical test one could apply. There are many other similar cases in our experience: Laurie Manns removed hundreds of pike from one large lake at the owner's request, the result was teeming hordes of pike with a high growth rate, but which never had time to grow up! Big pike *must* be handled carefully and returned.

Hotspots are something we have to live with. They are a *fact*, the effects of which pervade all aspects of pike angling. They are the reason why a serious pike angler cannot disclose the exact whereabouts of his successes, even when he believes, as we do, in supporting the angling press. No water in these islands has enough hotspots to withstand detailed publicity. Whilst hotspots cannot survive many anglers, particularly the bad handlers of pike, they can and do survive natural disasters of flood conditions, freeze ups and so on. Details of weather are important on your local water; fog being good for success on some, for example, and apparently bad on others. But barometric pressure probably affects overall control on the feeding of pike.

If you cannot beat the boat anglers, then join them, and whilst about it go afloat in Ireland and savour boat fishing at its most successful. It is essential to think as carefully about the boat itself as about the actual angling: its fitments, the angler's safety and the manipulation of the boat. Anglers who take to boats spend more time looking over the sides, than they do fishing from them.

The piker aware of all the foregoing, and awake to his own findings will, even though he be the country's worst caster, experience something of the lure of pike angling, and meet a whole succession of veritable gems of angling characters. As we said at one point this latter aspect may be at the core of one's enjoyment of fishing.

On page 210 is a blueprint for success and for enjoyment of the above: a kind of 'success can be yours' idea.